MISSION-ORIENTED
FINANCE FOR INNOVATION

About Policy Network

Policy Network is an international thinktank and research institute. Its network spans national borders across Europe and the wider world with the aim of promoting the best progressive thinking on the major social and economic challenges of the 21st century.

Our work is driven by a network of politicians, policymakers, business leaders, public service professionals and academic researchers who work on long-term issues relating to public policy, political economy, social attitudes, governance and international affairs. This is complemented by the expertise and research excellence of Policy Network's international team.

A platform for research and ideas

- Promoting expert ideas and political analysis on the key economic, social and political challenges of our age.
- Disseminating research excellence and relevant knowledge to a wider public audience through interactive policy networks, including interdisciplinary and scholarly collaboration.
- Engaging and informing the public debate about the future of European and global progressive politics.

A network of leaders, policymakers and thinkers

- Building international policy communities comprising individuals and affiliate institutions.
- Providing meeting platforms where the politically active, and potential leaders of the future, can engage with each other across national borders and with the best thinkers who are sympathetic to their broad aims.
- Engaging in external collaboration with partners including higher education institutions, the private sector, thinktanks, charities, community organisations and trade unions.
- Delivering an innovative events programme combining in-house seminars with large-scale public conferences designed to influence and contribute to key public debates.

www.policy-network.net

MISSION-ORIENTED FINANCE FOR INNOVATION

New Ideas for Investment-Led Growth

Edited by Mariana Mazzucato and Caetano C. R. Penna

policy network

ROWMAN &
LITTLEFIELD
—— INTERNATIONAL ——
London • New York

Published by Rowman & Littlefield International, Ltd.
Unit A, Whitacre, 26-34 Stannary Street, London, SE11 4AB
www.rowmaninternational.com

Rowman & Littlefield International, Ltd. is an affiliate of Rowman &
Littlefield
4501 Forbes Boulevard, Suite 200, Lanham, Maryland 20706, USA
With additional offices in Boulder, New York, Toronto (Canada), and
Plymouth (UK)
www.rowman.com

British Library Cataloguing in Publication Information Available
A catalogue record for this book is available from the British Library

ISBN: PB 978-1-78348-495-9

Library of Congress Control Number: 2015933672

ISBN 978-1-78348-495-9 (pbk. : alk. paper)
ISBN 978-1-78348-496-6 (electronic)

∞™ The paper used in this publication meets the minimum requirements
of American National Standard for Information Sciences Permanence of
Paper for Printed Library Materials, ANSI/NISO Z39.48-1992.

Printed in the United States of America

CONTENTS

Acknowledgements vii

About the Contributors ix

Introduction: Mission-Oriented Finance for Innovation I
 Mariana Mazzucato and Caetano C. R. Penna

PART I: HOW ECONOMISTS GOT IT WRONG – AN ALTERNATIVE DIAGNOSIS II

Fast Finance and Slow Growth 13
 Andrew Haldane

The Social Value of Finance: Problems and Solutions 21
 Adair Turner

How Maximising Shareholder Value Stops Innovation 31
 William Lazonick

Dispelling Myths about Government Deficits 39
 Randall Wray

PART II: WHAT GOVERNMENTS NEED TO DO TO CREATE REAL LONG-TERM GROWTH 49

Steering Economies Towards the Next Golden Age 51
 Carlota Perez

Why We Need Public Endowments for Transformative
    Research   59
    Arun Majumdar

Six Decades of Mission-Oriented Finance for
    Industrialisation, Technical Change and Innovation in
    Brazil   65
    Mariano Laplane

Challenges and Opportunities for a Knowledge-Based UK
    Economy   75
    Vince Cable

Why a Fundamental Shift in Innovation Policy Is Needed   85
    Tera Allas

PART III: LEARNING FROM SUCCESS AND FAILURE 95

Development, Uncertainty and the Role of State Investment
    Banks   97
    *Luciano Coutinho, João Carlos Ferraz and Felipe
    Silveira Marques*

Financing Energy Innovation: The Case of ARPA-E   105
    Cheryl Martin

The Rise of the State Investment Banks   111
    Matthias Kollatz-Ahnen

The European Investment Bank: Supporting Innovation in
    Europe   119
    Shiva Dustdar

The State as Venture Capitalist: The Case of the Danish
    Growth Fund   129
    Christian Motzfeldt

Financing Innovation: Lessons from Innovate UK   139
    Iain Gray

Conclusion: Beyond Market Failures: Shaping and Creating
    Markets for Innovation-Led Growth   147
    Mariana Mazzucato

ACKNOWLEDGEMENTS

This book is an outcome of a conference on Mission-Oriented Finance for Innovation (MOFI): Rethinking Public and Private Risks and Rewards, held in London on 22–24 July 2014. Speakers included leading policymakers, business executives and academics from 10 countries. This book is a collection of some of the key contributions, themes and discussions from the event.

The aim of the conference was to change the conversation – challenging conventional thinking about the role of the public sector in financing the innovation needed for smart, sustainable, inclusive growth. One of the key themes was the need to go beyond the 'market failure' framework in economic theory, and adopt a market creating/shaping framework, where the public and private sector are understood in terms of sharing both risk and rewards in the creation of new market and technological opportunities. Speakers reflected on the challenges and opportunities for an active public sector role, in addition to outlining the need for capacity and capability development within public institutions as much as in private ones. And the need to welcome the kind of experimentation process, full of trials and errors, that innovation requires in learning organisations.

The conference was organized by Mariana Mazzucato (SPRU, University of Sussex, UK) and Caetano Penna (SPRU) through Mazzucato's *Financing Innovation* research project, funded by the

Institute for New Economic Thinking (with Randall Wray as co-investigator, at the Levy Institute), as well as her *Entrepreneurial State* project funded by the Ford Foundation. The conference was sponsored by the Brazilian Development Bank (BNDES), with support from SPRU and the University of Sussex.

The book features the contributions from representatives of public agencies and leading academics in a condensed form. Their full speeches can be located on the conference website (www. missionorientedfinance.com), where other resources such as policy briefs, videos, and blogs can be found.

We would like to thank Policy Network for their enthusiastic backing of this project; Alison Rooper for editorial work; and Gemma Smith for communications assistance and for coordinating the various actors involved. We thank all the sponsors and panellists for their contributions. We are especially grateful to Vince Cable, UK secretary of state for business, innovation and skills, for hosting the first day of the conference in the UK parliament; Matthew Taylor, chief executive of the Royal Society for the Encouragement of Arts, Manufactures and Commerce, for opening the second day at the RSA; and Kit Malthouse, deputy mayor of London for business and entrepreneurship, for hosting the third day in London's glorious City Hall. Finally, we thank Luciano Coutinho, João Ferraz and their team at BNDES for their support and continued interest in this project.

Mariana Mazzucato and Caetano Penna
30 January 2015

ABOUT THE CONTRIBUTORS

Tera Allas is former director general (strategic advice, science and innovation leadership) at the UK Department for Business, Innovation and Skills and former deputy head of the government Economic Service. She serves as a strategic and economic advisor to a number of governmental, business and third sector organisations internationally, and previously held chief economist positions at the UK Department for Transport and the Department of Energy and Climate Change. Prior to this, she worked for 10 years as a management consultant at McKinsey & Company, focusing on corporate and business unit strategy and corporate finance. She holds an MSc in technology and industrial economics (with distinction) from Helsinki University of Technology and an MBA (with distinction) from INSEAD, France.

Vince Cable is UK secretary of state for business, innovation and skills and MP for Twickenham. He studied natural science and economics at Cambridge University, followed by a PhD at Glasgow University. He served in the Liberal Democrat shadow cabinet as spokesman on trade and industry (1999–2003), shadow chancellor (2003–2010), and deputy leader of the Liberal Democrats (2006–2010). Cable worked as Treasury finance officer for the Kenyan government in the 1960s as well as in a range of senior academic, economic and foreign policy roles before becoming Shell International's chief economist in 1995.

Luciano Coutinho is president of the Brazilian Development Bank BNDES. He is a specialist in competition law, international trade, and macroeconomic and market forecasting, and winner of the Brazilian-American Chamber of Commerce's Person of the Year 2013 award for his outstanding work in forging closer ties between the two countries.

Shiva Dustdar is head of research, development and innovation advisory at the European Investment Bank, Luxembourg. She was previously in its risk management directorate and then in its EU lending directorate, where she was responsible for the financing of R&D projects using the Risk Sharing Finance Facility. Before joining the EIB in 2003, she worked at Fitch Ratings as director of high yield, and from 1993 to 1999 at J.P. Morgan in its M&A Advisory team in New York as well as in its Investment Banking Group in London.

João Carlos Ferraz is managing director of the BNDES and an economist, specialising in comparative development, industrial economics and public policies. He is currently on leave from his positions as professor of economics at the Economics Institute of the Federal University of Rio de Janeiro and senior economist at the United Nation's Economic Commission for Latin America and the Caribbean.

Iain Gray was chief executive of Innovate UK (formerly the UK Technology Strategy Board) from 2007 to 2014. After joining BAE Systems as a structures engineer in 1979, he served as head of engineering, and, from 2006, managing director of Airbus UK. He is a chartered engineer, a fellow of the Royal Academy of Engineers and a fellow of the Royal Aeronautical Society. In 2007 he was awarded the Royal Aeronautical Society Gold Medal and in 2011 he was elected as a fellow of the Royal Society of Edinburgh.

Andrew G. Haldane is chief economist at the Bank of England and executive director of monetary analysis and statistics. A member of the Bank's monetary policy committee, he also has responsibility for research and statistics across the Bank. In 2014, *Time* magazine voted him one of the 100 most influential people in the world. Haldane has written extensively on domestic and international monetary and financial policy issues. He is co-founder of Pro Bono Economics, a charity that brokers economists into charitable projects.

Matthias Kollatz-Ahnen was appointed as finance senator for the state government of Berlin in December 2014. Previously, he was senior expert at PricewaterhouseCoopers, Germany. From 2006 to 2012 he was a senior vice-president of the European Investment Bank, with responsibility for its lending programmes in Turkey, Germany, Austria, Romania and Croatia. He is a former managing director and a member of the management boards of the Investitionsbank Hessen (Hesse Investment Bank) and the Landes Treuhandstelle Hessen (the Hesse State Trust Agency).

Mariano Laplane is the president of the Center for Strategic Studies and Management, a social organisation affiliated to the Brazilian Ministry of Science, Technology and Innovation. He is also associate professor at the Institute of Economics of the State University of Campinas, where he heads the graduate study programme. He has an MA in city planning from the University of California, Berkeley, and a PhD in economics from UNICAMP. He is a member of the Mercosur Economic Research Network based in Montevideo.

William Lazonick is a professor of economics at the University of Massachusetts Lowell, where he directs the Center for Industrial Competitiveness. He is co-founder and president of the Academic-Industry Research Network (the AIRnet). He is also a visiting professor at the University of Ljubljana and the Telecom School of Management, Paris. Previously, he was assistant and associate professor of economics at Harvard University; professor of economics at Barnard College of Columbia University; and distinguished research professor at INSEAD, France. He also holds an honorary doctorate from Uppsala University.

Arun Majumdar is a professor at Stanford University in the faculty of the department of mechanical engineering and a senior fellow of the Precourt Institute for Energy. He was formerly vice-president for energy at Google. From 2009 to 2012 he served as the first director of the US Advanced Research Projects Agency–Energy (ARPA-E), the country's only agency devoted to transformational energy research and development. He also served as the US acting under-secretary of energy. Previously, he was associate laboratory director for energy and environment at Lawrence Berkeley National Laboratory and a professor of mechanical engineering and materials science and engineering at the University of California, Berkeley.

Felipe Silveira Marques is assistant to the BNDES president and an economist, specialising in the economics of information and communication technologies, holding a PhD from the Economics Institute of the Federal University of Rio de Janeiro.

Cheryl Martin is deputy director of the Advanced Research Projects Agency–Energy (ARPA-E) at the US Department of Energy where she leads ARPA-E's Technology-to-Market programme, which helps breakthrough energy technologies succeed in the marketplace. Prior to joining ARPA-E, she was an executive in residence with the venture capital firm Kleiner Perkins. She also spent 20 years with Rohm and Haas Company, starting her career as a senior scientist for the company's Plastics Additives business.

Mariana Mazzucato holds the R.M. Phillips Chair in the Economics of Innovation at SPRU in the University of Sussex. Her recent book, *The Entrepreneurial State: Debunking Private vs. Public Sector Myths*, was featured on the 2013 Books of the Year lists of the *Financial Times* and *Forbes*, and it focuses on the need to develop new frameworks to understand the role of the state in economic growth – and how to enable rewards from innovation to be just as 'social' as the risks taken. She is winner of the 2014 New Statesman SPERI Prize in Political Economy and in 2013 the *New Republic* called her one of the "three most important thinkers about innovation". She advises the UK government and the European commission on innovation-led growth. Her research outputs, media engagement and talks (including her TED Global talk) can be found on her website (www.marianamazzucato.com).

Christian Motzfeldt is the chief executive officer at the Danish Growth Fund (Vækstfonden). Before this, he served in the Danish Ministry of Industry and Trade, where his last position was that of deputy permanent secretary in charge of business economics. Prior to 1994, he worked at Danske Bank, the Danish national bank, and the European commission.

Caetano C. R. Penna is research fellow at the Institute of Economics of the Federal University of Rio de Janeiro (Brazil). He received his BA in economics from the Federal University of Rio de Janeiro and his MA in Technology Governance from Tallinn University of Technology. He holds a PhD in Science and Technology Policy Studies from SPRU in the University of Sussex, where he previously worked as research fellow. Together with Mazzucato, he has developed the video project *Rethinking the State*. He is a founding partner of BabelTeam Internet Business Solutions.

Carlota Perez is centennial professor of international development at the London School of Economics; professor of technology and development at the Nurkse Institute, Technological University of Tallinn; and honorary professor at SPRU, University of Sussex. Her book, *Technological Revolutions and Financial Capital: The Dynamics of Bubbles and Golden Ages*, has contributed to the present understanding of the relationship between technical and institutional change, finance and economic development.

Adair Turner is a senior fellow at the Institute for New Economic Thinking and at the Centre for Financial Studies in Frankfurt. He became chair of the UK Financial Services Authority as the financial crisis broke in September 2008 and played a leading role in the redesign of the global banking and shadow banking regulation as chair of the International Financial Stability Board's major policy committee. Prior to 2008 he was a non-executive director at Standard Chartered Bank; vice-chair of Merrill Lynch Europe; and director general of the Confederation of British Industry. He is a member of the House of Lords.

Randall Wray is a professor of economics at the University of Missouri–Kansas City and senior scholar at the Levy Economics Institute of Bard College. His current research focuses on providing a critique of orthodox monetary theory and policy and the development of an alternative approach. He also publishes extensively in the areas of full employment policy and, more generally, fiscal policy. With Dimitri B. Papadimitriou, he is working to publish, or republish, the work of the late financial economist Hyman P. Minsky, and is using Minsky's approach to analyse the current global financial crisis.

INTRODUCTION

Mission-Oriented Finance for Innovation

Mariana Mazzucato and Caetano C. R. Penna

Six years have passed since the collapse of Lehman Brothers kicked off what later became the most severe economic crisis since the Great Depression. Governments, political parties and different elements of civil society across the globe remain locked in debate over what to do with regard to government debt levels, fiscal deficits and public investments. Typically, this wrangling over the size of deficits has prevented a focus on the composition of public spending and the type of institutions that guide it. At best, we hear the need to spend on 'infrastructure' and 'shovel-ready projects'.

Yet, in a period when major economies are still reeling from the aftershocks of the crisis and struggling to face up to the grand societal challenges of our time – climate change, the ageing crisis, youth unemployment – the emphasis of this book is on the need for public policy to make a step change: shaping and creating markets for long-term economic growth, and, in doing so, learning from 'mission-oriented' investments of the past which were able to direct investments towards transformational areas. It was, indeed, such investments that brought us the IT revolution – and could bring us in the near future the 'green revolution' that has the potential to transform sectors across the world.

Amid the debate between parties on what should or should not be cut to keep down levels of public debt, it is fundamental to ask how the choices made about public spending and investment today will affect the future growth that will help increase the supply of funds available to both private and public investment in the future. This, in fact, is what is crucial: the problem is not the deficit, but what it is being spent on, so that GDP (the denominator of debt to GDP) can grow in the long run. Indeed, in some countries (like Italy), deficits have been low; yet debt-to-GDP levels have skyrocketed precisely because productivity and GDP have not been growing, which, in turn, is due to the lack of both public and private investments in key areas like human capital formation and R&D. So, the big question is what to spend on so that long-term GDP can grow, which, over time, will decrease the debt-to-GDP levels even with modestly rising deficits.

It is here that our book begins: what can we learn from such investments in the past? How were they directed? Did they aim to fix a narrow set of problems or to transform future landscapes?

PUBLIC INVESTMENT: CREATING AND SHAPING MARKETS, NOT ONLY FIXING THEM

Those regions and countries that have succeeded in achieving smart innovation-led growth have benefited from long-term visionary mission-oriented policies – from putting a man on the moon to tackling societal challenges such as climate change.[1] In addressing these missions, public sector agencies have led the way, investing not only in the classic 'public good' areas, like basic research, but also along the entire innovation chain (basic research, applied research, early-stage funding of companies) and courageously defining new high-risk directions. Traditional cost-benefit analysis and market failure justifications would have halted these investments from the outset[2]: there would have been no internet, no biotech, no nanotech, and, today, no cleantech. Thinking about governments and public investments as mission-oriented lets us move the debate on fiscal policies forward.

Instead of focusing on *ad hoc* infrastructure investments in new highways and railroads, a mission-oriented government considers transformational changes – such as the development of new general purpose technologies – that affect all sectors. This is not an easy task. To fulfil this mission-oriented function, state agencies – ranging from public banks like KfW in Germany and BNDES in Brazil[3] to innovation agencies like DARPA and ARPA-E in the US and Innovate UK in the UK – have been willing to explore new landscapes, tackling extreme uncertainty, accepting the trial and error process that often leads to failures, with the successes leading potentially to decades of growth: well worth the wait. How do they do it? What challenges lie ahead? Should government step back or step up? And how can we socialise both risks and rewards so that economic growth is not only smart but also inclusive?

Of course, public investment cannot operate alone. It is dependent on an engaged, committed private sector willing to share the burden, especially in downstream areas. Is 'financialisation' of the real economy causing companies to worry more about their stock prices than future growth opportunities, and hence threatening such engagement? If so, how can mission-oriented innovation policies also promote de-financialisation by addressing targeted, strategic public investments alongside transformations in corporate governance and financial market reform?

This book provides an insight into these questions with contributions from practitioners from some of the most important mission-oriented agencies around the globe, as well as from leading economists placing their actions in the context of a world in transition, which requires deep transformations.

MISSION-ORIENTED FINANCE FOR INNOVATION

The types of public sector organisations represented in this book share a crucial feature: they are concerned with innovation-driven growth – smart growth. As Joseph Schumpeter[4] argued decades ago, it is only this kind of growth that results in truly economic development. And economists following on his tradition have shown that tomorrow's growth – or long-term economic growth – is determined by today's investments in R&D, infrastructure projects, human capital, technical change and innovation.[5] But innovation requires decisions on directionality and capabilities to understand and engage dynamically with future technological and market opportunities. This book's contributions highlight the diversity of roles performed by public sector organisations in the innovation process, the way that directions have been steered, public-private partnerships built and the perception of the challenges and new missions that countries face in the current economic environment. The goal of the book is to open up the debate on the role of the state in the innovation process, moving beyond fixing market failures. The key insights stem from a three-day conference entitled Mission-Oriented Finance for Innovation, which was held in London on 22–24 July 2014.[6] The book seeks to foster a lasting impact of the ideas discussed, opening the conversation with key stakeholders worldwide.

Alongside the contributions from the policymakers, interspersed in the book are chapters by leading economists who challenge the prevailing narrative about economic growth. In the spirit of Karl Polanyi's *The Great Transformation*,[7] their emphasis is on the need for public policy to actively create and shape markets, not only to fix them. Randall Wray of Levy Economics Institute of Bard College explains the role of money in capitalist economies, the process of funding economic development and where public finance for innovation comes in a post-Keynesian new money theory perspective. The importance of public finance for innovation and the risk-taking role of the state contrasts with the central pillars of the 'maximising shareholder value' theory, which William Lazonick of the University of Massachusetts deconstructs. He argues that the real patient capitalists are not the shareholders – but taxpayers, workers and investors in real assets. But even if private financiers and investors were willing to provide patient finance to the real economy, would this be enough? This is the question addressed by Carlota Perez of the London School of Economics, who suggests that more would be needed, in the form of a new shared direction, vision or mission that would stir innovation, investments and, ultimately, economic development towards a new 'golden age'. She proposes that the new mission is 'green growth', which goes beyond addressing climate change or saving the planet: it implies a redefinition of the aspirational 'good life' towards the health of the individual and the environment. Mariana Mazzucato of SPRU at the University of Sussex concludes by pulling together the lead themes in the book, changing the discourse about the role of the public sector in the economy, outlining four key questions that can help public agencies and departments to 'think big' again.

The book is structured in three parts. The first part focuses on the current context: a world in which the financial crisis has turned into a full-blown economic crisis which many countries are struggling to overcome. Finance is key to this first section, providing a different diagnosis of what is (still) wrong with financial markets and their relationship with the real economy six years after the outbreak of the 'great recession'. It opens with a contribution by Andrew Haldane of the Bank of England on how the socioeconomic and individual focus on the short term impairs economic growth and development. Short-termism is one of the key features of our financial system, which is, for instance, concerned with speculative investments in stocks or real estate. Such issues are discussed in detail by Adair Turner in his chapter 'The Social Value of Finance: Problems and Solutions'. William Lazonick then steps back and argues that the problem is not just the short-termism of finance, and its lack of financing of the real economy, but the degree to which the real economy itself has become financialised. The first part ends with a contribution by Randall Wray, who connects the discussion back to the way in which a transformation of the financial system can help to break down myths about the role of governmental deficits.

The second part captures what is missing from the current limited, deficit-cutting discourse in the UK, the US and across Europe: asking politicians to think boldly about the kind of investment needed to deliver future growth. Why? Because history shows us that addressing the major challenges facing society requires patient, targeted mission-oriented finance to foster the radical innovations that lead to tomorrow's growth. This is the argument put forth by Carlota Perez, who discusses what can be done by the state in order to avoid another Great Depression (as in the 1930s) and to foster a new golden age of capitalism (as in the 1950s and 1960s). This chapter is complemented by the contributions from Arun Majumdar, Mariano Laplane, Vince Cable, and Tera Allas. Majumdar, a professor at Stanford University who previously worked at ARPA-E and Google Energy, defends the importance of public endowments for transformative research, such as the public investments that led to the ICT revolution and are currently promoting renewable energy innovations.

Mariano Laplane, who works in a leading Brazilian agency that provides consultancy service to the Brazilian Ministry of Science, Technology and Innovation, reviews six decades of mission-oriented finance for industrialisation, technical change and innovation in Brazil. Vince Cable, Britain's secretary of state for business, innovation and skills, discusses what the UK government is doing, and should do, to promote mission-oriented innovations and economic growth. While further funding announcements have been made since his conference speech was first delivered, the overall strategic agenda which he promotes gives a strong flavour of his view that financial market reform and innovation policy must go hand in hand.

Concluding the second part of this book, Tera Allas, former director general, strategic advice, science and innovation leadership in the UK government's Department for Business, Innovation and Skills, argues that a fundamental shift in governments' approach to financing innovation is needed: to think big and stop immaterial activities; prioritise and focus to ensure clear directionality; take an end-to-end perspective and coordinate across boundaries; and build the structures and capabilities to deliver truly strategic interventions.

Indeed, a common theme is the need to build public organisations that welcome failure, exploration, trial and error, and serendipity. And yet, this is required if we want public finance for innovation. So the third part of the book documents the way that successful, mission-oriented public agencies around the world are operating and the challenges they face. It starts with a chapter by Luciano Coutinho, the president of the Brazilian development bank, BNDES. Together with his colleagues he discusses the role of development finance institutions in the absorption of risks and uncertainties that underlies the innovation and economic development process. In the following chapter Cheryl Martin, deputy director of ARPA-E, discusses how institutions can be mission-oriented by accepting risks and using failures as opportunities to learn: failures will always happen, so mission-oriented public agencies need to welcome them. Matthias Kollatz-Ahnen, former vice-president of the European Investment Bank (EIB), discusses the key characteristics that allow some development (or promotional) banks to be successfully mission-oriented. His contribution is complemented by the chapter by Shiva Dustdar, head of research, development and innovation at EIB, who discusses how the EIB promotes innovation in Europe through innovative financial instruments.

Public risk-taking is the prerogative of another key type of public financial institution: public venture capital funds. Christian Motzfeldt presents the case of one of the most important mission-oriented public venture capital funds in Europe, the Danish Growth Fund, which he leads as chief executive officer. The third part of the book ends with the contribution by Iain Gray, until recently director of Innovate UK (formerly the Technology Strategy Board), who argues that the role of public institutions concerned with financing innovation is to direct public investment towards the big challenges: what he calls missions or 'races'.

Mariana Mazzucato's call for policymaking and public agencies to move beyond the limited focus on addressing market failures, and instead to engage in shaping and creating markets through investments in research and development, innovation and technological change that address the grand societal challenges of our time, concludes the book. She argues this requires rethinking four pillars: directionality of investments; their evaluation and assessment; public organisations willing to take risks; and the distribution of risks and rewards.

As a whole, this book highlights the fundamental transformations that are required in order to change the economic policy discourse from a narrow one, focused on deficits and spending, to a broader one, on directionality and strategic investments. What we need is a discussion on how to redirect the economy towards sustainable long-term growth, and the type of government investments that are needed to achieve this. In order to do so it is fundamental for public policymakers to think big again, guided by mission-setting agendas, directed not only at 'public goods' but also a public purpose to fundamentally transform existing landscapes and create the future technological and market opportunities that can drive future decades of growth. This requires public sector institutions to welcome the trial-and-error process of exploration that is needed for learning organisations, and to embrace what Albert Hirschman[8] called 'policy as process'.

The contributions to this book are a powerful argument for a fundamental step change: enabling us to build creative dynamic public organisations of the future, so that public-private partnerships are not only about the 'de-risking' side of public policy but also about courageously sharing both risks and rewards.

Mariana Mazzucato holds the R.M. Phillips Chair in the Economics of Innovation at SPRU in the University of Sussex. Her recent book, *The Entrepreneurial State: Debunking Private vs. Public Sector Myths*, was featured on the 2013 Books of the Year lists of the *Financial Times* and *Forbes*, and it focuses on the need to develop new frameworks to understand the role of the state in economic growth – and how to enable rewards from innovation to be just as 'social' as the risks taken. She is winner of the 2014 New Statesman SPERI Prize in Political Economy

and in 2013 the *New Republic* called her one of the "three most important thinkers about innovation". She advises the UK government and the European commission on innovation-led growth. Her research outputs, media engagement and talks (including her TED Global talk) can be found on her website (www.marianamazzucato.com).

Caetano C. R. Penna is research fellow at the Institute of Economics of the Federal University of Rio de Janeiro (Brazil). He received his BA in economics from the Federal University of Rio de Janeiro and his MA in Technology Governance from Tallinn University of Technology. He holds a PhD in Science and Technology Policy Studies from SPRU in the University of Sussex, where he previously worked as research fellow. Together with Mazzucato, he has developed the video project *Rethinking the State*. He is a founding partner of BabelTeam Internet Business Solutions.

NOTES

1. Mazzucato, M. (2013) *The Entrepreneurial State: Debunking the Public Vs. Private Sector Myths in Risk and Innovation.* London: Anthem Press; Mowery, D. C. (2010) 'Military R&D and Innovation', in Hall, B.H. & Rosenberg, N. (eds.) *Handbook of the Economics of Innovation*, 1219–56.

2. Mazzucato, M. (2014) *Building the Entrepreneurial State: A New Framework for Envisioning and Evaluating a Mission-Oriented Public Sector,* Levy Institute Working Paper no. 824.

3. Mazzucato, M. and Penna, C. (2014) *Beyond Market Failures: The Market Creating and Shaping Roles of State Investment Banks,* SPRU Working Paper Series, 2014-21, http://www.sussex.ac.uk/spru/documents/2014-21-swps-mazzucato-and-penna.pdf.

4. Schumpeter, J. A. (1934 [1912]) *The Theory of Economic Development: An Inquiry into Profits, Capital, Credit, Interest, and the Business Cycle. Harvard Economic Studies.* Cambridge, Mass.: Harvard University Press.

5. Verspagen, B. (2005) 'Innovation and Economic Growth', in Fagerberg, J., Mowery, D.C. & Nelson, R.R. (eds.) *The Oxford Handbook of Innovation*. Oxford: Oxford University Press, 487–513.

6. Mission-Oriented Finance for Innovation, http://missionoriented finance.com.

7. Polanyi, K. (1944) *The Great Transformation: The Political and Economic Origins of Our Time*. Beacon Press.

8. Hirschman, A.O. (1982) *Shifting Involvements: Private Interest and Public Action*. Princeton University Press.

Part I

How Economists Got It Wrong – An Alternative Diagnosis

FAST FINANCE AND SLOW GROWTH

Andrew Haldane

Consider two countries – China and Italy. As recently as 1990, these economies were equal in size as measured by aggregate GDP at purchasing power parity exchange rates. But let us now put these countries on quite different trajectories for capital accumulation. Let China begin investing at double-digit rates for 20-plus years, while Italy accumulates capital at a rate of only two per cent per year. By 2013, China is now seven times larger than Italy. Indeed, China is creating an economy the size of Italy's every two years; an economy the size of Greece's every quarter; and an economy the size of Cyprus's every week.

GDP may not be all that matters, as economists are increasingly coming to accept. But, as these figures suggest, it nonetheless matters a lot if we care about improvements in living standards over lengthy time spans.

GROWTH IN THE LONG TERM

Societies are accustomed to becoming better off, generation by generation. Yet, looking across the span of human history, this has often not been the case. Measures of global GDP have been constructed back to 1 million BC. Statistical agencies were thin on the ground back then, so these numbers need to be treated with an even greater degree of caution than today's GDP releases. Nonetheless, the secular patterns they reveal are striking.

Up to around 50,000 BC, as best we can tell, world GDP per capita was essentially unchanged. Generation after generation, there was little – if any – improvement in living standards. Things improved, progressively, after that. By 1750 AD, world GDP per capita had almost doubled, having risen at a heady rate of 0.0025 per cent per year. Today's economists would call that an anaemic recovery. But for perhaps the first time in human history, living standards were at least now rising.

From 1750 AD onwards, the world entered a third growth era; a golden era. Since then, GDP per capita has risen 40-fold, at an annual rate of around 1.5 per cent per year. On average, each generation has been perhaps one third better off than its predecessor. So what explains these phase shifts in growth?

HOW HUMANS DEVELOPED PATIENCE

There is no one explanatory factor, but one key element is what sits between our ears. Something important neurologically happened to humans around 50,000 years ago. Neanderthal man died out and homo sapiens became dominant. That meant prominent brow ridges were replaced by high, straight foreheads. And they did so for a reason – namely, to accommodate growth of the prefrontal cortex region of the brain.

Modern neurology tells us that this part of the brain is responsible for patience, the ability to defer gratification. It is the part crucial for investment. In primitive societies, this meant investment in the very basics of survival – food, water, shelter, defence – but also in the institutions which helped sustain these basics: families, communities, tribes, civilisations.

After 1750 AD, the great leaps forward were in one sense different – industrial rather than agrarian. Yet they had essentially the same mix of physical, human, and social capital accumulation underpinned by a new set of institutions – schools, governments, judicial systems, even central banks. Patience generated investment, and investment, in turn, generated growth.

The important work of Daron Acemoglu and James Robinson[1] has recently shown that societies that have not invested in institutions have tended to fail. In other words, institutions – the organisational form of patience – are crucial for societal development.

What these historical episodes demonstrate, above all else, is the importance of one very basic human and societal attribute in generating rising living standards: patience – the willingness to defer gratification, to build physical, human, and social capital, to create and sustain institutions, and to innovate.

WHAT PATIENT PEOPLE DO

Patience, we are told, is a virtue. But recent evidence has demonstrated just how much of a virtue. For example, we know that patient people are, predictably enough, more likely to save than spend. They are also more likely to stay on in higher education, to have a job, to vote, to join a gym, to save on energy. Most interestingly, cross-country evidence suggests that patient societies are also more technologically innovative.

So, given its importance to innovation and growth, you might ask: what factors determine the patience of individuals and societies? We now know quite a bit about this too. Several individual and societal characteristics are important, including gender, income, wealth, and age. So, too, are long-term cultural values. Unfortunately, none of these factors are easy to change, at least quickly.

But there is one further factor, every bit as important, which is amenable to change: the environment for decision-making. Importantly, this includes the role of government and other institutions in nurturing patient decision-making. For example:

- by creating *incentives* to save and invest rather than spend;
- by creating *institutions* that promote education and skills;

- by creating *infrastructures* that support innovation; and
- by providing *nudges* which shape long-term behaviour, be it attending a gym or saving on energy.

FAST FOOD AND FAST THOUGHT

Let me illustrate the importance of even small interventions on patient decision-making with an example that is at the same time both trivial and profound. A few years ago some psychologists[2] assessed how individuals' decision-making was affected by sending subliminal images of two iconic 21st century fast-food images – the 'golden arches' from McDonalds and Colonel Sanders from Kentucky Fried Chicken. These cues, despite not even entering people's consciousness, had a dramatic impact on measured levels of patience: the mere subliminal sight of Colonel Sanders raised people's one-year discount rates by around a third. Fast food made for fast thought.

The deeper point here is that time-saving technologies, including fast food, are meant to nurture patience by stretching time. In practice, they appear to have done the opposite, encouraging the fast-thinking part of the brain. And it is not just fast food. The most important time-saving technology of our lifetime – the web – is believed by some to have induced a neurological bias towards short-term decision-making. Be it the rise in payday lending and attention deficit disorders or falling levels of job and marital tenure, there are signs that society may be becoming more impatient.

SHORT-TERMISM AND FINANCE

From fast food, then, to fast finance. Many of these societal trends are evident, in amplified form, in finance. Modern capital markets rarely give the impression of valuing the long term; they delight in profits being distributed rather than reinvested.

Take public equity markets. These, and the accompanying rise of the public limited company, were one of the great financial innovations of the 19th century. Why? Because, as a perpetual instrument, public equity ought to be ideal for financing long-term investment, be it railways, or car manufacturers, or software houses. And for perhaps a century that is just what it did.

Yet, today, the omens are not encouraging. Fifty years ago, the average share was held by the average US investor for around seven years. Today, it is seven months. Equity contributes almost nothing to the net new financing of UK companies. McKinsey & Company has argued that global equity markets may be entering a long-term period of decline. [3]

That naturally begs the question – why? The short answer, it seems, is short-termism. Investors in public equity markets value too little long-term projects yielding distant returns, and too much the instant gratification of dividends or stock buy-backs. The upshot is that companies are put off from investing in those long-horizon, high-risk, high-innovation projects in the first place.

IRRATIONAL INVESTORS

In my own research, I have tried to estimate this short-termism bias in public equity markets. On average, returns one year ahead appear to be discounted around 5–10 per cent 'too much'. That may not sound like much, but it can have a dramatic effect on long-term project choice.

Imagine a project that provides an annual income stream of $10 and requires a $60 initial outlay. If the 'true' discount rate is eight per cent, this project earns a positive net present value (NPV) within a decade. A rational company would undertake it. But with excess discounting of 10 per cent per year, investors believe the project would never break even. The project would never be financed by public equity markets.

If this irrationality was confined to financial markets, it perhaps would not matter much. Unfortunately, it is not. Surveys of company chief executives and CFOs indicate that they turn down positive NPV projects because of the need to keep short-term investors sweet. Studies comparing privately owned and publicly traded companies indicate the former may invest more than twice the latter.

Over time, these differences would translate into a material impact on the capital stock and growth. A rough back-of-the-envelope calculation for the UK suggests that output could be up to 20 per cent higher without these short-termism biases. That is a whole generation's worth of growth.

PATIENT CAPITAL

The final question, then, is how best to create this better environment for patient capital and growth. From a potentially long list, let me offer three areas I think are ripe for reform.

Reforming Taxation and Regulation

For example, why does the tax code, globally, continue to bias against equity and towards debt? This, too, was a 19th century invention that may have outlined its usefulness. It is, in effect, a tax on long-termism.

As for financial regulation, this may embed some of the same incentives – for example, regulation of pension fund and insurance companies. As long-term institutions, they are ideally placed to finance long-term investment. Yet regulation in practice tends to attach higher regulatory charges to longer-duration instruments, even though they may do a better job of supporting growth. If you like, regulation weighs risk but not return.

Risk-based regulation and accounting rules tend also to weigh more heavily when the market slumps. This, perversely, is when patient capital is often most needed. Ideally, we would want long-term investors to act counter-cyclically, stepping in to take on risk when it is cheap. More often, it appears, the opposite is happening.

The good news is that some reorientation of regulation is underway. Regulation is taking on a more *macro*-prudential dimension.

Think of it as regulating for the needs of the real economy, for return as well as for financial risk. Macro-prudential regulation aims explicitly to support long-term, diverse sources of financing, and it also aims to dampen, not amplify, financial cycles.

As one example of that, the Bank of England and European Central Bank recently initiated a joint programme to stimulate securitisation markets in Europe, including for SMEs. This should increase the diversity of the financial system, with more long-term financing coming from long-term institutions. As another example, the Bank has recently lowered the bar for new entrants into the banking market, to encourage greater competition and diversity.

Institutions that Nudge

You would expect someone who has spent their whole working life in a 320-year-old institution to tell you how important they are. And in fact, in an increasingly impatient society, their role has never been more important. National and multi-national development banks are testament to the power of patient state-backed institutions in catalysing investment, innovation, and growth. And here in the UK, the British Business Bank and Green Investment Bank have similar aspirations.

But this catalytic role for institutions extends much beyond direct financing. It is also about providing the right nudges and prompts for innovation. Another experimental study, similar in spirit to the fast food one, looked at the impact of subconscious images of two company logos: IBM and Apple. People shown the Apple logo exhibited much greater levels of creativity than those shown the IBM logo. A subliminal nudge was sufficient to catalyse innovation. Institutions can create that creativity nudge at a societal level.

Reforming the PLC

That great 19th century innovation, the PLC, placed power in the hands of shareholders because they were there for the long term.

Yet, today, those same shareholders are unrecognisable, their holding periods and long-term incentives much diminished.

This poses a challenge to the PLC model, at least as operated in
the UK and US. Giving primacy to the interests of short-term shareholders may come at a cost – the cost of short-termism, suboptimal-
ly high hurdle rates, a failure to invest and innovate. Shareholders
today may be part of the short-termism problem.

Some corporate governance models lean against this bias, explicitly recognising the interests of a broader set of stakeholders – debt
holders, workers, customers, suppliers, wider society. On average,
these corporate governance models appear to have done a better job
of sustaining investment and nurturing innovation. For macroecono-
mists, their success should come as no surprise. As China shows,
long-term investment holds the key to future growth.

**Andrew G. Haldane is chief economist at the Bank of England
and executive director of monetary analysis and statistics. A
member of the Bank's monetary policy committee, he also has
responsibility for research and statistics across the Bank. In
2014, *Time* magazine voted him one of the 100 most influential
people in the world. Haldane has written extensively on domestic and international monetary and financial policy issues. He is
co-founder of Pro Bono Economics, a charity that brokers economists into charitable projects.**

NOTES

1. Acemoglu, D. and Robinson, J. A. (2012) *Why Nations Fail: The
Origins of Power, Prosperity and Poverty.* New York: Crown Publishers.

2. Zhong, C.-B. and DeVoe, S. E. (2010) 'You Are How You Eat: Fast
Food and Impatience', *Psychological Science,* 21(5), 619–22.

3. McKinsey (2010). *Farewell to Cheap Capital? The Implications of
Long-term Shifts in Global Investment and Saving.* Available at http://
www.mckinsey.com/insights/global_capital_markets/farewell_cheap_
capital; accessed on 15/11/2014.

THE SOCIAL VALUE OF FINANCE: PROBLEMS AND SOLUTIONS

Adair Turner

How do we stop the financial system from occasionally blowing up the world and producing – as it has post-2007/2008 – a severe post-crisis recession? Let me start with the fact that finance has got much bigger. Over the last 50 years, finance has come to play a far bigger role in modern advanced economies. In the 1950s the total finance sector in the US accounted for about 2.5 per cent of GDP; by 2007, that was about eight per cent of GDP. There is a very similar growth pattern in the UK. In other countries the absolute figures are often smaller, but the direction of change is the same.

FINANCE IN OUR ECONOMY IS THREE TIMES BIGGER THAN IT WAS IN THE 1950s

Why is that? There are two dominant elements. One is that real economies became more leveraged. They borrowed more money. So if you take all the advanced economies together, in the early 1950s they had private sector debt to GDP of about 50 per cent, and by 2007 that had grown to 170 per cent. So the size of what the financial system did vis-a-vis the real economy in the debt markets had become much bigger. There had to be more money, more deposits, more bonds, more fixed-interest instruments of some sort.

The other reason why finance got much bigger is that it did far more trading with itself. It created a set of instruments that were intensively used within the financial system itself, such as derivatives.

So if you take a whole series of indices that relate a financial activity to a real economy activity, you get a dramatic increase in those ratios; you get far more foreign exchange trading relative to the value of actual real trade; you get an explosion of derivatives that had not previously existed; and, in particular, you get a change in shape of the balance sheets of the major international banks.

HOW BANK BALANCE SHEETS CHANGED

If you looked at the biggest banks of the world back in the 1950s, an ordinary person could understand them because, broadly speaking, on both the asset and the liability side there was a set of assets which were claims on households, companies, and governments, and on the liabilities side there was a set of liabilities to households and companies. But if you were to look at the balance sheet of Goldman Sachs, or Deutsche Bank, or Barclays today, you would discover that the majority of the balance sheet is a set of claims vis-a-vis other parts of the financial sector. It is Barclays to Deutsche Bank. It is Deutsche Bank through Goldman Sachs, with a huge explosion of derivatives activities, trading activities, interbank activities.

Was it good that finance got so much bigger relative to real economy? Finance is very different from the real economy. It is very different because it is not a consumer good valued in itself; it is valuable if it is performing functions with regard to the real economy and performing them well. It connects savers and investors. It has a crucial role in the mobilisation and the allocation of capital. So it is crucial for us to ask the question: is it doing this as cost efficiently and as effectively as possible?

PRAISE FROM THE ECONOMISTS FOR THE SYSTEM

Before the crisis in 2007, the predominant point of view of finance and macroeconomic theory expressed in many books and articles was very positive about the growth of the financial system. And the story that was told was broadly a very positive story about this process of financialisation and financial deepening. It had three elements.

First, there was a very strong assertion that markets in financial instruments are efficient and rational, and that they are more efficient the more liquid they are; that liquid equity markets achieve efficient processes of price discovery as defined by the efficient market hypothesis, and that the more liquid they are, the more trading they are, the more efficiently they do this.

Second, it was very strongly argued that debt contracts were a good thing because they enabled a mobilisation of capital that might not occur if every investment in the economy had to take an equity fall. If when you invested in a project you had to take an equity investment, you would not have invested so much. People, companies, or households, in particular, wanted the certainty of debt contracts, of what the economists called 'non-state contingent contracts'.

Third, there was an argument that what had occurred in the arena of securitisation, credit structuring, and derivatives was that we had extended to the credit and debt markets the advantages of liquid trading and transparent prices, which we had always had in equity markets. And so it was a good thing that we had taken debt contracts off the liquid books of banks and turned them into liquid traded credit securities, which then – the story was – could be allocated round the economy and end up in the hands of the investors best placed to absorb the specific risk and return of specific securities that had been tailored to more precise combinations of risk and return by the glories of securitisation collateralised debt obligations (CDOs), and, of course, which could be hedged by the glories of credit default swaps (CDSs).

And the assertion was that those changes had not only made the financial system more efficient by doing its job of capital mobilisation and allocation more efficiently, but that it had also made the financial system, and therefore the macroeconomy, more stable.

If you read the IMF global financial stability review of April 2006, only 15 months before the biggest financial crisis in modern capitalism, you will read a paean of praise to the great glories in which structured credit, and derivatives, and trading, and shadow banking have made the financial system more stable.

QUESTIONING ECONOMIC ORTHODOXY

Seen from my point of view of stability and why the macroeconomy goes wrong, we have to question that orthodoxy after 2007 and 2008 in lots of different ways – first in relation to equity markets or liquid traded markets in total. I do not believe in the efficient market hypothesis. I fundamentally believe that the things that are true about the efficient market hypothesis are trivial and the things that could be important are untrue.

I think that all liquid traded markets are subject to herd effects, to irrational effects of the type that Robert Shiller and George Akerlof[1] and others have written about, and that that has a set of consequences for the role of liquid traded markets and for other bits of the ecosystem of finance – such as venture capital – in the processes of capital allocation. The role of equity markets, of whether they serve long-term purposes, is something which Mariana Mazuccato[2] and others have written about.

The third point, I think, was also totally wrong. In retrospect, the developments of shadow banking, of securitisation of derivatives and all the supposedly sophisticated risk management and trading mechanisms that we put in place, far from making the system more stable, essentially took the dangerous potential instability of the credit and asset price cycle and hardwired and turbocharged it.

TEXTBOOKS ARE WRONG ABOUT BANKS

Were we right to consider that the growth of credit to GDP was a good thing? What do textbooks tell us about bank credit within the economy? If you pick up an economics undergraduate book, what it says is this: Banks take deposits, savings from households, and they lend it to businesses/entrepreneurs to finance capital investment projects, thus achieving both an intermediation of saving and an efficient allocation between alternative capital investment projects.

The problem with that description of what banks do – and a problem right at the core of understanding financial instability – is that those words are completely mythological. And, indeed, they are wrong in two fundamental senses. Banks do not just take existing money and savings and intermediate it; they create money, credit, and purchasing power in the way that the Austrian economists such as Ludwig van Mises and Joseph Schumpeter and Friedrich Hayek described. And so, obviously, the question of whom they give that new purchasing power and credit to, who is empowered with new credit, is absolutely fundamental to the dynamics of the economy. But the second way in which they are mythological is in believing that most bank credit is extended to businesses/entrepreneurs to fund new capital investment projects: that is not what banks do in the modern world.

BANKS AND REAL ESTATE

Banks can do at least two other things: they can lend money to consumers, either in a mortgage form or in an unsecured form to bring forward consumption in the lifecycle (which could be welfare-enhancing if it optimally smooths consumption across the lifecycle within a permanent income constraint), and also, crucially, they can finance a competition for the ownership of assets that already exists. That can be, for instance, in the private equity market, where much of what private equity does is offer not venture capital or new capital investment, but leveraging up against assets which already exist.

By far, the biggest element of where banks do this leveraging up against existing assets is in real estate.

Economist Alan Taylor and his colleagues have analysed 17 major advanced-economy banking systems over the last 140 years, and their conclusion was quite simple: "with very few exceptions the banks' primary activity up to the 1920s and even the 1970s was non-mortgage lending to business but by 2007 banks in most countries had turned primarily into real estate lenders."[3] The intermediation of household savings for productive investment in the business sector constitutes only a very minor share of what modern banking systems do today. Thus, banks are not primarily doing what the textbooks say they do.

Now, that, of course, at the very least suggests that we should change the textbooks, but it also raises the question as to whether we should change the banks. Should we try and turn them back to what they were 50 years ago – which was lending money to businesses? I do not want to leap immediately to that conclusion, because I also suggest that we are not going to get rid of it, and we must not attack it too much.

Modern economies are bound to become more real estate-intensive over time. As people get richer they will tend to reach satiation in many categories of consumption, and one thing they will do with an increasing proportion of their rising income is compete more aggressively for the right to live in the nice part of town, for the nice bits of real estate, and effectively for the limited supply of urban land on which that real estate sits. So I think it is almost inherent that modern economies become more real estate-intensive. Banks or the capital markets are bound to do a significant amount of real estate lending. But we need to equally recognise that banks are likely to become more focussed on real estate than is socially optimal, with adverse macroeconomic and microeconomic effects.

WHY WE STILL HAVE A WEAK RECESSION

Real estate lending has proved to be the overwhelmingly predominant driver of financial crises and macroeconomic instability.[4] And this, I believe, is the fundamental reason why in 2014, six years after 2008, we are still struggling with a weak and slow recession. It is not the weakness of the banks. It is the fact that we have overleveraged households and companies who got overleveraged in real estate. And real estate lending has an adverse economic and social effect; but it is an adverse social and economic externality because, seen from the point of view of the individual bank or credit security investor, it can appear to look low risk and can actually be low-risk, even while it is producing those adverse collective effects.

Bank lending to real estate also appears to be a simpler, easier, cheaper thing than any other form of lending because you can credit-score it, or you can simply lend on a loan-to-value basis. By contrast, lending to a business that does not have real estate assets is tricky, expensive, requires analysis of the business activity, and can be risky. Left to itself, the banking system will overprovide credit for real estate purchase and for real estate investment, and will underprovide credit for business investment, business development, and business innovation. And that justifies public policy interventions, both to constrain and manage overall levels of credit and to produce a different allocation of credit than a purely free market model would produce.

DIFFERENT SOLUTIONS FOR DIFFERENT PROBLEMS

I want to end by suggesting that policy interventions might lie in three different places, depending on the problem we are trying to solve.

If the problem is that there is not enough credit to small and medium enterprises in general – whether or not they are innovators – we could change the capital risk weights within the banking system. We could set higher capital requirements against real estate lending to reflect the social externality of real estate lending, which no individual, private banker will ever take into account.

Suppose, however, point two: that we were worried not about general business development but about innovation and funding breakthroughs in science and technology. Then I suspect that we have to be willing to step in with actual direct government support or specific government guarantees, rather than simply playing around with the risk weights.

Finally, suppose we were worried about infrastructure development – not the breakthroughs in solar energy but who is going to fund the installation of large-scale solar energy or the installation of large-scale wind energy. Here it is less immediately obvious why there should be a market failure. The crucial issue here is about risk and return. One thing that the public sector can do, whether it be through development banks, or through guarantees, or through the design of utility regulation, is take risk off the table – because the public sector is a better manager of risk – and get down the cost of infrastructure finance, even if that infrastructure finance comes from the private sector.

Are we talking about general business development, about technological innovation per se, or about infrastructure development? I think the policy levers will differ, but the background – at least in relation to debt – is this: do not rely on the private sector, left to itself, to end up in a socially optimal space. The private sector, left to itself, will gravitate inevitably, not only to the necessary element of real estate finance, but also to far too much real estate finance than makes sense in a socially optimal fashion. Those, therefore, are three questions with which I end up.

Adair Turner is a senior fellow at the Institute for New Economic Thinking and at the Centre for Financial Studies in Frankfurt. He became chair of the UK Financial Services Authority as the financial crisis broke in September 2008 and played a leading role in the redesign of the global banking and shadow banking regulation as chair of the International Financial Stability Board's major policy committee. Prior to 2008 he was a non-

executive director at Standard Chartered Bank; vice-chair of Merrill Lynch Europe; and director general of the Confederation of British Industry. He is a member of the House of Lords.

NOTES

1. Shiller, R. (2000) *Irrational Exuberance*, Princeton: Princeton University Press; Shiller, R. and Akerlof, G. (2009) *Animal Spirits: How Human Psychology Drives the Economy, and Why It Matters for Global Capitalism.* Princeton: Princeton University Press.

2. Mazzucato, M. (2013) 'Financing Innovation: Creative Destruction vs. Destructive Creation', *Industrial and Corporate Change,* 22(4), 851–67; Mazzucato, M. and Shipman, A. (2014) 'Accounting for Productive Investment and Value Creation', *Industrial and Corporate Change,* 23(4), 1059–85.

3. Jordà, Ò., Schularick, M. and Taylor, A. M. (2014) 'The great mortgaging: housing finance, crises, and business cycles', *NBER Working Paper*, 20501. Available at http://www.nber.org/papers/w20501, downloaded on 13/11/2014.

4. This is well argued by Claudio Borio, economist at the Bank for International Settlement, in Borio, C. (2012) *The Financial Cycle and Macroeconomics: What Have We Learnt?*, BIS Working Paper No. 395, December 2012. Available at http://www.bis.org/publ/work395.htm; accessed on 12/11/2014.

HOW MAXIMISING SHAREHOLDER VALUE STOPS INNOVATION

William Lazonick[1]

Whenever financial markets get hyperactive (the norm rather than exception over the past three decades), we hear calls for 'patient capital' that can fund long-term investment in the productive capabilities that are essential for a prosperous economy. In particular, it is said that those who have control over the allocation of the economy's resources are afflicted by 'short-termism'. What the pundits invariably mean is that investors in productive capabilities have to be willing to wait long periods of time before demanding financial returns from them. But these admonitions are often vague about what functions patient capital performs, and who stands to benefit from it.

Innovation – the process that generates the higher-quality, lower-cost products that enable productivity growth – is collective and cumulative. It takes lots of people and lots of time to develop the productive capabilities that become embodied in the new processes and products that can raise our standards of living.

WHY INNOVATION NEEDS PATIENT CAPITAL

Innovation is collective because in order to generate higher-quality, lower-cost products, the skills and efforts of people with an array of functional capabilities and hierarchical responsibilities must be integrated into organisational learning processes. It is cumulative because what the collective can learn today depends on what it learned yesterday. Collective and cumulative (or organisational) learning is needed to transform technologies and access markets. That is how our economy gets productivity growth.

Even if learning were individual, it would still be cumulative. Learning that is collective tends to be more powerful in transforming technologies and accessing markets because it integrates skills and efforts in a functional and hierarchical division of labour. This collective learning requires a social condition of innovative enterprise that I call 'organisational integration'.

If innovation cannot be done all alone, it also cannot be done all at once. Patient capital sustains this collective and cumulative learning process from the time at which investments in it begin to be made to the time when – through the generation of a higher-quality, lower-cost product than was previously available – innovation can produce the revenues that provide financial returns. This cumulative learning requires a social condition of innovative enterprise that I call 'financial commitment'.

Besides organisational integration and financial commitment, the innovative enterprise requires a third social condition: 'strategic control'. Investments in innovation are inherently uncertain. Those executives who exercise strategic control over the allocation of resources must have the abilities and incentives to invest in innovation in the face of uncertainty. If, at the outset of the learning process, we knew how to generate a higher-quality, lower-cost product, it would not be innovation!

THE UNCERTAINTIES OF INNOVATION

Investors in innovation face three different types of uncertainty: technological, market, and competitive. Technological uncertainty exists because it may prove impossible to develop the high-quality product that the innovative strategy envisions. Market uncertainty exists because even if the enterprise generates the intended high-quality product, it may not be able to access the extent of the market necessary to drive down unit costs to competitive levels. And competitive uncertainty exists because it is always possible that a rival will generate an even higher-quality, lower-cost product. Yet if a business enterprise does not make investments in innovation in the face of uncertainty, it cannot hope to be an innovative enterprise.

The type of organisational integration and the extent of financial commitment that is required for a potentially effective investment in innovation will depend on three things: first, the characteristics of the technologies to be developed; second, the types of markets to be accessed; and third, the existence of competitors that may be able to innovate better, faster, and cheaper than your firm. Indeed, in some industries the amount of patient capital needed is so great, and the duration of time over which that capital must be patient is so long, that only the government is virtuous enough to make the financial commitment needed to set an innovation process in motion.

The need for such 'mission-oriented' finance is not an exceptional case. Virtually every sophisticated technology that we now routinely put to use had its origins in such government investment projects.

HOW THE US GOVERNMENT HAS USED PATIENT CAPITAL

For at least a century and a half, the exemplar in making these patient investments has been the US government. If you know some US history, just think of railroads, public universities, agricultural science, electrification, aeronautics, medical science, interstate highways, computers, the internet, and a host of specific technologies related to the ongoing information-and-communication technology revolution. (Unfortunately, the same people who extoll hyperactive financial markets because of the 'liquidity' that they provide seem to be the same people who do not know much about history.)

Governments, however, are not usually in the business of ensuring that the productive capabilities in which they have invested taxpayer money get transformed into goods and services that, when sold to buyers, actually generate financial returns. The purpose of government agencies is to invest in infrastructure and knowledge that, funded directly or indirectly by taxpayer money, society needs to have available. The purpose of business enterprises is to produce competitive products: goods or services that buyers need or want at prices that they are able or willing to pay. Even then, when there are goods and services that households need at prices that most of them are unable to pay, the government often subsidises either the businesses that supply the products or the households that demand them.

With government investments and subsidies in place, the innovative business enterprise requires a combination of strategic control, organisational integration, and financial commitment to address, respectively, the uncertain, collective, and cumulative character of the innovation process. The abilities of those executives who exercise strategic control over the allocation of the firm's resources shape their visions of the characteristics of both potentially innovative products and the learning processes needed to transform potential into reality. The incentives of these executives affect whether, in the face of uncertainty, it is even in their personal interests to allocate the firm's resources to innovative investments.

HOW US EXECUTIVES EXTRACT EXCESS VALUE FOR THEMSELVES

'Impatient capital' occurs when those who exercise strategic control within a business enterprise seek to use these positions of power to

	Mean Total Direct Comp. $m.	Mean Total Direct Comp. 2013 $m.	Salary	Bonus	Non-Equity Incentive Plan	All Other Comp	Deferred Earnings	Realized Stock Option Gains	Realized Stock Award Gains
2006	27.4	30.8	3.3	7.0	7.6	5.9	0.5	58.9	16.8
2007	30.0	32.9	3.0	4.1	6.9	7.6	0.1	58.8	19.6
2008	22.9	24.6	4.1	4.2	8.7	4.1	0.1	43.9	34.9
2009	14.4	15.4	7.0	4.8	14.9	7.4	0.1	39.9	25.9
2010	18.5	19.5	5.5	4.8	15.0	6.2	0.1	40.3	28.1
2011	19.4	20.0	5.5	4.8	15.0	6.2	0.1	40.3	28.1
2012	30.3	30.8	3.6	2.7	8.2	3.2	0.1	41.5	40.7
2013	32.2	32.2	3.3	1.9	7.6	3.5	0.1	55.4	28.2

Figure 3.1. Compensation Paid to Top-Paid Executives in the US (*Source*: Standard and Poor's ExecuComp database, with calculations by Matt Hopkins, The Academic-Industry Research Network)

reap financial rewards for themselves that are not warranted by the productive contributions that they have made to generating higher-quality, lower-cost products; that is, the value that they extract exceeds the value that they have helped to create. In most nations, led again by the US, the way in which those who exercise strategic control extract excess value is through stock-based remuneration. Figure 3.1 shows the total remuneration and its various components of the 500 highest-paid executives in the US, as reported in company proxy statements for the years 2006–2013. The realised gains from stock options and stock awards accounted for 66 per cent to 84 per cent of total remuneration.

It is not only in established companies that executives reap outsized rewards. Research in which I am engaged with Öner Tulum and Mustafa Erdem Sakinç of The Academic-Industry Research Network shows that even at companies that have never generated a commercial product and yet have been listed on the public stock market (a common characteristic of firms in the US biopharmaceutical industry), executives often reap millions of dollars in stock-based pay.

HOW STOCK PRICES ARE MANIPULATED

How do they do it? A company's stock price reflects a combination of innovation, speculation, and manipulation. When stock market traders see that a company has become profitable through innovation, they bid up its stock price. Speculation about future profits often follows, pushing stock prices up further. Powerful players may then find ways to manipulate stock prices. For example, highly visible stock market traders may spread unsubstantiated rumours about a company's prospects that can boost stock prices further (or in the case of short-selling, push them down).

But as my research has shown, top corporate executives of established companies do not leave it to stock market traders to manipulate their stock prices. They can do it themselves through stock buybacks. Over the decade 2004–2013, about 9,000 US companies expended a total of $6.9tn on stock buybacks. That was 43 per cent of their combined net income, with dividends absorbing another 47 per cent. Companies in the S&P 500 Index did about half of the buyback total. The 454 companies included in the S&P 500 Index in March of 2014 that were publicly listed from 2004 through 2013 expended $3.4tn on buybacks, equal to 51 per cent of net income, and another $2.3tn on dividends, 35 per cent of net income. And buybacks remain in vogue: for the 12-month period ending September 2014, S&P 500 companies spent $567bn on buybacks, up 27 per cent from the previous twelve-month period.

Their stock-based pay gives these executives the incentive to allocate corporate resources to manipulate their companies' stock prices. And the Securities and Exchange Commission, the US agency that is supposed to prevent manipulation of the stock market, lets them do it under Rule 10b-18, promulgated in 1982 as part of the Reaganite deregulation of the economy. Legitimising this massive extraction of corporate cash is the pervasive ideology, also a product of the 1980s, that, for the sake of superior economic performance, a company should be run to 'maximise shareholder value' (MSV).

THE FALSE MANTRA OF 'MAXIMISING SHAREHOLDER VALUE'

MSV assumes that all shareholders invest in the firm's productive assets, and that of all the participants in the business enterprise, it is only shareholders who bear the risk of profit or loss on the investments in the productive assets of the firm. Both of these assumptions are wrong. The vast majority of shareholders trade in the outstanding shares of publicly listed companies, making no investment at all in the firms' productive assets. These shareholders only risk the loss of the value of the shares that they buy, and with a liquid stock market, they can rid themselves of that risk instantaneously at minimal transaction costs.

In contrast, households, as taxpayers through various government agencies, invest in physical infrastructure and human knowledge that are vital to the ability of firms. And workers as firm employees engaged in processes of organisational learning expend their time and effort in improving the productive capabilities of the enterprise. Both taxpayers and workers bear risk that they will receive low or no returns on these investments in the firm's productive assets.

Through the tax regime, the body of taxpayers should be able to reap returns from taxes on individuals and companies that profit from the investments in the productive assets of firms. But those profits may not be forthcoming, and even when they are, the wealthy often use the political process to lower taxes on themselves, often invoking MSV to justify their claims. Through career employment with a company, workers who invest in organisational learning should reap returns from innovation in the forms of employment stability and higher pay. But the innovation process may not be successful, and even when it is, these employees may be laid off – again, typically in the name of MSV. As investors in the firm, taxpayers and workers take risk because they have no guarantee of reaping returns, even when profits are forthcoming.

THE REAL PATIENT CAPITALISTS

These taxpayers and workers, along with financiers who make investments in the firm's productive resources and reap returns only when the firm generates profits from innovation, are the real patient capitalists. Moreover, 'impatient capitalism' cannot be attributed to 'short-termism'. Rather, it represents the use of power by those who control the allocation of corporate resources to shift the rewards of innovative enterprise away from households as taxpayers and workers to themselves. This value extraction without value creation represents a prime cause of the concentration of income at the top and the loss of middle-class jobs. Patient capital is a virtue because it rewards the real value creators in the economy, providing a foundation for stable and equitable economic growth.

William Lazonick is a professor of economics at the University of Massachusetts Lowell, where he directs the Center for Industrial Competitiveness. He is co-founder and president of the Academic-Industry Research Network (the AIRnet). He is also a visiting professor at the University of Ljubljana and the Telecom School of Management, Paris. Previously, he was assistant and associate professor of economics at Harvard University; professor of economics at Barnard College of Columbia University; and distinguished research professor at INSEAD, France. He also holds an honorary doctorate from Uppsala University.

NOTE

1. Documentation of the arguments in this chapter can be found in research papers available at www.theAIRnet.org.

DISPELLING MYTHS ABOUT GOVERNMENT DEFICITS

Randall Wray

The Mission-Oriented Finance for Innovation conference explored how to direct funding toward what Hyman Minsky called "the capital development of the economy", broadly defined to include private investment, public infrastructure, and human development. But to understand how, we need to understand what money is and why it matters. After all, finance is the process of getting money into the hands of those who will spend it.

The dominant narrative in economics is that money 'greases' the wheels of commerce. Sure, you could run the commercial machine without money, but it runs better with lubricant.

In that story, money was created as medium of exchange: instead of trading your banana for her fish, you agree to use cowry shells to intermediate trade. Over time, money's evolution increased efficiency by selecting in succession unworked precious metals, stamped precious metal coins, precious metal-backed paper money, and, finally, fiat money comprised of base metal coins, paper notes, and electronic entries.

However, that never changed the nature of money, which facilitates trade in goods and services. As Milton Friedman famously argued, in spite of the complexity of our modern economy, all of the important economic processes are revealed in the simple Robinson Crusoe barter-based economy.

Money is a 'veil' that obscures the simple reality; in the conventional lexicon, money can be ignored as 'neutral' (for those well versed in economics, we need only refer to the Modigliani-Miller theorem[1] and the efficient markets hypothesis that 'proved' finance does not matter).

We worry about money only when there is too much of it: Friedman's other famous claim is that "inflation is always and everywhere a monetary phenomenon"; that is, too much money causes prices to rise. Hence all the worry about the Federal Reserve's quantitative easing, which has quadrupled the 'Fed money' (reserves) and by all rights should be causing massive inflation. This chapter will provide a different narrative, drawing on Joseph Schumpeter's notion that the banker is the 'ephor' – or overseer – of capitalism.

WHY THE DOMINANT ECONOMIC NARRATIVE IS WRONG

Looking at money from the perspective of exchange is highly misleading for understanding capitalism. In the Robinson Crusoe story, I have a banana and you have a fish. But how did we get them? In the real world, bananas and fish have to be produced – production that has to be financed. Production begins with money to purchase inputs, which creates monetary income used to buy outputs. As any mother insists, 'money doesn't grow on trees'. How did producers get money in the first place? Maybe by selling output? Logically, that is an infinite regress argument – a 'chicken-and-egg' problem. The first dollar spent (by producer or consumer) had to come from somewhere.

There is another problem. Even if we could imagine that humanity inherited 'manna from heaven' to get the monetary economy going – say, an initial endowment of one million dollars – how do we explain profits, interest, and growth?

If I am a producer who inherited $1000 of manna, spending it on inputs, I am not going to be happy if sales are only $1000. I want a return – maybe 20 per cent, so I need $1200. If I am a moneylender, I lend $1000 but want $1200, too. And all of us want a growing pie. How can that initial million manna do double and triple duty?

BANKERS AS THE OVERSEERS OF THE SYSTEM

Here's where Schumpeter's 'ephor' comes in. An ephor is 'one who oversees', and Schumpeter applied this term to the banker. We do not need to imagine money as manna, but rather as the creation of purchasing power controlled by the banker.

A producer wanting to hire resources submits a prospectus to the banker. While the banker looks at past performance as well as wealth pledged as collateral, most important is the likelihood that the producer's prospects are good – called 'underwriting'. If so, the ephor advances a loan.

More technically, the banker accepts the IOU of the producer and makes payments to resource suppliers (including labour) by crediting their deposit accounts. The producer's IOU is the banker's asset; the bank's deposits are its liabilities but are also the assets of the deposit holders (resource suppliers). This is how 'money' really gets into the economy – not via manna from heaven or Friedman's 'helicopter drops' by central bankers.

When depositors spend (perhaps on consumption goods, perhaps to purchase inputs for their own production processes), their accounts are debited, and the accounts of recipients are credited. This circular flow is captured by a simple model of how money is created, with a single bank (see Figure 4.1).

THE ROLE OF THE CENTRAL BANK

Today, most 'money' consists of keystroked electronic entries on bank balance sheets. Because we live in a many-bank environment,

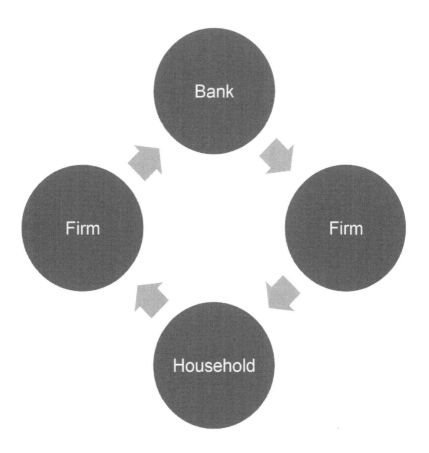

Figure 4.1. A Simple Model of Money (Single Bank) (*Source*: Author's construction)

payments often involve at least two banks. Banks clear accounts by debiting claims against one another, or by using deposits in correspondent banks. However, net clearing among banks is usually done on the central bank's balance sheet (see Figure 4.2).

Like any banker, the Fed or the Bank of England 'keystrokes' money into existence. Central bank money takes the form of reserves or notes, created to make payments for customers (banks or the national treasury) or to make purchases for its own account (treasury securities or mortgage-backed securities). Bank and cen-

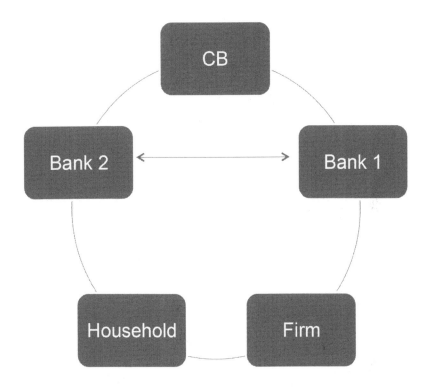

Figure 4.2. A Simple Model of Money (Multiple Banks) (*Source*: Author's construction)

tral bank money creation is limited by rules of thumb, underwriting standards, capital ratios, and other imposed constraints.

THE MYTH ABOUT GOVERNMENTS 'RUNNING OUT OF MONEY'

Most developed countries have adopted constraints on sovereign spending that are widely believed to stop government from just 'creating money' to finance spending. The two most common requirements are: that the treasury must have deposits in its account at the central bank before it can spend; and that the treasury cannot borrow directly from the central bank (that is, by selling bonds to the central bank) to get those funds.

Many people believe (wrongly) that these are effective constraints against 'printing money' by the sovereign. What they do not understand is that the central bank – from its very creation – has always been the treasury's bank. It makes all payments for the treasury, and receives all payments to the treasury (most importantly, tax payments); moreover, it can no more run out of 'central bank money' than private banks can run out of their own 'bank money'. In both cases, the payments are made by keystrokes.

When the treasury wants to purchase something from a contractor, it sends an order to the central bank to debit the treasury's account and to keystroke a credit to the reserves of the private bank (bank 1 in Figure 4.3, in this case). The bank then keystrokes credits to the deposit account of the contractor. When taxpayers write cheques to the treasury to pay taxes, their banks (bank 1, in this case) debit their accounts and make tax payments for them, using their own reserve deposits at the central bank. The central bank, in turn, debits bank reserves and credits the treasury's deposit account at the central bank.

That is fine and dandy, but what if the treasury wants to spend but has already drawn down its account at the central bank? Well, we know that the central bank never bounces a treasury cheque for lack of funds. If it did, you can bet that the central bank's governor will be called in by the head of the administrative branch (president or prime minister) for a good lecture!

WHY TREASURY CHEQUES DO NOT BOUNCE

How is that avoided? The easiest way would be for the central bank to grant 'overdraft' facilities for the treasury. In practice, there are sometimes prohibitions on this – probably in the mistaken belief that by ruling out overdrafts, the treasury will be constrained. However, it should be noted that in times of war or crisis, the rule against overdrafts is often overruled.

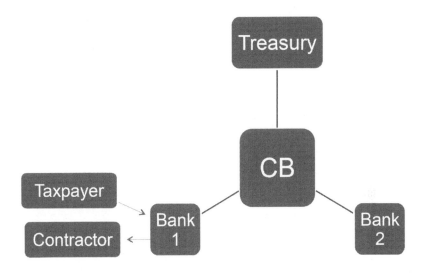

Figure 4.3. A Simple Model of Money (Multiple Banks and Treasury)
(*Source*: **Author's construction**)

One must remember that on any given day the treasury receives hundreds of thousands or even millions of tax payments, and makes just as many payments. It is impossible to predict how much will be received in payments, and how many treasury cheques will be presented for payment on any day. In the US, the Fed and treasury communicate each morning to make projections for the day's payments, receipts, and net balances. However, those projections will (inevitably) be off.

How does the treasury deal with errors? Well, one way is to keep a positive balance in its account (just as you do); however, in practice, that balance is quite small. Tax receipts tend to come in bunches, while payments are more evenly spread (although concentrated around the beginning of months). And if the treasury is running a deficit (as almost all treasuries do), it will consistently find itself short.

For these reasons, the central bank and treasury have developed procedures to ensure there are always 'funds in the account'; these procedures include creating relations with special banks that receive payments for the treasury, and special dealer banks that stand ready to always purchase treasury securities. When the treasury expects to be 'short', it moves funds from these special banks to the central bank, and sells securities to special dealer banks.

The central bank also cooperates by ensuring these banks have access to reserves that are needed to shift deposits or to buy treasury securities. If necessary, the central bank lends reserves (or allows 'float', which is just a type of overdraft). And if the banks decide they do not want to hold treasury securities, they sell them on to the central bank that stands ready to buy them in the 'open market'.

This effectively undermines the prohibition that prevents treasury from selling securities to the central bank, since they are sold round about through the banks and hence on to the central bank.

What many people forget is that the central bank has two over-riding concerns. First, it needs the payments system to operate smoothly – and that means that it does not want cheques to bounce, which would undermine par clearing. Above all, the government's own cheques must clear. Bouncing government cheques would quickly cause fear and panic.

Second, it wants to hit its overnight interest rate target (the Fed funds rate, or bank rate). That means it must accommodate bank demand for reserves – including reserves banks need to cover treasury operations (transfers from tax and loan accounts, purchases of treasury securities).

All of this gets technical, but the proof that the central bank and treasury know what they are doing is in the pudding, so to speak. In spite of the complexity, treasury cheques do not bounce, and the central bank does hit its interest rate target (within a margin of error that is discretionary).

WHY GOVERNMENT DEFICITS NO LONGER MATTER FOR SOVEREIGN SOLVENCY

Even in the case of Japan – which has an outstanding government debt-to-GDP ratio of more than 2.5 to 1, and the biggest sustained budget deficits the world has ever seen – the operations run smoothly, with treasury cheques clearing and the Bank of Japan keeping overnight rates essentially at zero.

So when we hear politicians proclaiming 'the government has run out of money', as Barack Obama has done on many occasions, or was said by the UK coalition government when it assumed office in 2010, we can be sure that they are wrong. Sovereign government cannot run out of its own keystrokes.

After abandoning the gold standard, there are no physical limits to money creation. We cannot run out of keystroke entries on bank balance sheets – whether we are talking about private banks or the government's central bank. This recognition is fundamental to issues surrounding finance. It is also scary.

The good thing about Schumpeter's ephor is that sufficient finance can always be supplied to fully utilise all available resources to support the capital development of the economy. We can keystroke our way to full employment.

THE DANGERS OF FUELLING ASSET PRICE BUBBLES

The bad thing about Schumpeter's ephor is that we can create more funding than we can reasonably use. Further, our ephors might make bad choices about which activities ought to get keystroked finance.

It is difficult to find examples of excessive money creation to finance productive uses. Rather, the main problem is that much – or even most – finance is created to fuel asset price bubbles. And that includes finance created both by our private banking ephors and by our central banking ephors.

The biggest challenge facing us today is not the lack of finance, but rather how to push finance to promote both the private and the public interest – through the capital development of our country. How can we use finance to promote the capital development of the economy?

FINANCE IS NOT A SCARCE RESOURCE

Finance is not a scarce resource – whether we are talking about finance coming from our private banks or central bank finance of our sovereign government. We can have as much as we want.

The problem in recent years has been that our governments wrongly think they are financially constrained, while our private financial system has been directing much of its efforts to self-enrichment rather than to capital development.

To move forward, we need to dispel the dual myths that government has run out of money and that the unfettered invisible hand of finance will promote the public interest.

Randall Wray is a professor of economics at the University of Missouri–Kansas City and senior scholar at the Levy Economics Institute of Bard College. His current research focuses on providing a critique of orthodox monetary theory and policy and the development of an alternative approach. He also publishes extensively in the areas of full employment policy and, more generally, fiscal policy. With Dimitri B. Papadimitriou, he is working to publish, or republish, the work of the late financial economist Hyman P. Minsky, and is using Minsky's approach to analyse the current global financial crisis.

NOTE

1. The Modigliani-Miller theorem (after economists Franco Modigliani and Merton Miller) states that, under certain market conditions, the value of a firm depends only on the income stream generated by its assets and is therefore unaffected by how that firm is financed (the share of debt in its financial structure). See Villamil, A.P. (2008) 'Modigliani-Miller Theorem', in Steven N. Durlauf and Lawrence E. Blume (eds.), *The New Palgrave Dictionary of Economics Online*, Palgrave Macmillan. Available at http://www.dictionaryofeconomics.com/article?id=pde2008_M000187; accessed on 19/7/2014.

Part II

What Governments Need to Do to Create Real Long-Term Growth

STEERING ECONOMIES TOWARDS THE NEXT GOLDEN AGE

Carlota Perez

My participation in the Mission-Oriented Finance for Innovation project has aimed to initiate the necessary dialogue between the financial advisers and policymakers and those who advise technology and innovation policies.

I look at the problem from the perspective of the projects that seek investment and in the context in which they are formulated and assessed. The issue is the following: supposing companies in the stock market and finance became willing to fund long-term projects. That would indeed be wonderful. But would it be enough to bring a robust revival of the economy? I suggest not.

As we all know, many of those allocating the money currently available for investment are not choosing between short- or long-term projects in the real economy, but between the real economy and the financial casino – often with moral hazard. At the same time, we are witnessing employment shifts and a strong polarisation of income. This is directly linked to the intense financialisation of the economy that has historically accompanied the initial decades of diffusion of a new technological paradigm, and the major bubbles that result.

Long-term data gathered by Thomas Piketty and Emmanuel Saez[1] on US income distribution among taxpayers shows how similar the polarisation in the recent bubbles is to that of the 'roaring 20s' (see Figure 5.1). Both periods of extreme income inequality are in stark contrast with the resulting reversal in the post-war boom, when suburbanisation, the cold war and mass production innovation brought jobs and growth, while officialised labour unions, the tax structure and the welfare state ensured that the incomes of the majority of citizens increased with productivity.

In fact, these major bubbles and the economic disruptions that they cause have occurred five times since the first Industrial Revolution of the 1770s brought the first great surge of industrial development to England. When we examine history more closely, we see that such bubbles are part of the process of technological advance, which is not continuous, but rather has occurred in five technological revolutions to date (see Figure 5.2). Each of those great surges of development unleashes a whole set of powerful new industries and

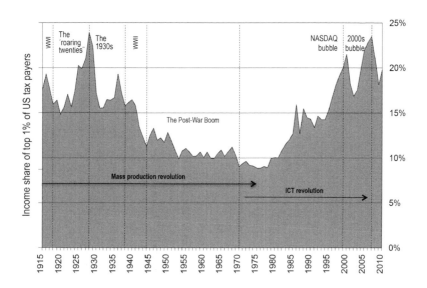

Figure 5.1. How Financialisation Polarises Income During Major Bubbles (*Source*: Piketty and Saez [2010], *op. cit.* [period indications by the author])

infrastructures: a new techno-economic paradigm, enabling a quantum leap in productivity for all industries, widening and deepening market spaces, shifting the centres of industrial dynamism and changing the rankings in world power.[2]

As Figure 5.2 shows, historically the golden ages have come after the major bubble collapses, using the technologies that were installed during the bubble prosperity. Thus, while our current information and telecommunications technology revolution has enabled a new global techno-economic paradigm, its full transformative impact on society is still to be defined. The opportunity we face today happens only once or twice in a century, midway along the life of each technological revolution. We are now in the equivalent of the 1930s, not in terms of depression but in terms of future potential. The available potential now is as enormous as it was then and is as invisible. It can enable innovation across all sectors of the economy: old, new, and to be created.

But it is only a potential. For despite the regular, cyclical nature of these technological revolutions, the outcome of these great

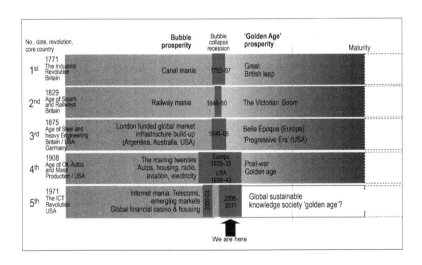

Figure 5.2. The Historical Record: Bubbles, Recessions and Golden Ages (*Source*: **Author's construction**)

changes for the economy and for society is far from predetermined. Sociopolitical choices make a huge difference. While long-term investment is essential, it will only become attractive and profitable if it is in a synergistic context.

As we try to emerge from the bubble collapse and recession, information-communication technology is already providing part of that context and, indeed, that is the main enabler of profitable innovation today. But the deployment of a technological potential – as it occurs in the later decades of diffusion – is not the same as the shift to a new technoeconomic paradigm, when the revolution is in its initial decades. There need to be many projects with a similar technological and market bias across many different industries, if we want to create technology systems (with common services, specialised suppliers, skills and user habits). That is how the necessary synergies and externalities will be created, to attract further projects in the same direction as well as complementary activities and business models. Very often it is these induced activities that create the most jobs. History shows that the high-productivity industries often create the best jobs but not necessarily the most jobs.

Thus, although the industries of a technological revolution are self-propelled and generate their own synergies, when they are to transform all the other sectors in the economy (which is why we call them revolutions), they need to have a direction for a converging transformation.

That is what can be understood by 'mission-oriented' innovation. The challenge can be as narrow as a man-on-the-moon or as wide-ranging as a suburban-home-for-all, as in the 1950s and 1960s. In the late 19th century, when the age of steam and steel brought the first globalisation, procurement for weaving the global transport and telegraph networks for naval, military and trade purposes served as the powerful generator of synergies for innovators and investors.

Yet having a common direction involves sociopolitical choices. It requires not a 'level' playing field – as pure-market advocates would recommend – but actually tilting the playing field in a clear direction so that the real economy becomes the most profitable option. Controversially, it means that the market cannot be relied upon for choosing the general direction of change.

The problem is that a lot of what is technologically feasible faces very high market and profit risks – as we have seen with renewable energies. This means that the projects currently considered for investment – short- or long-term – are only a fraction of what could be available. And with both shareholders and venture capital favouring short-termism – and finding easier and bigger gains in casino finance – the projects funded are a fraction of that fraction.

TILTING THE PLAYING FIELD

So, how do we get out of that trap? As unpalatable as the idea may be to some, the state must step in to tilt the playing field – as it has done in the past following every major bubble collapse. How was it done in the 1940s to unleash the post-war boom? By a set of institutional and financial innovations steering investment and innovation in two main directions: suburbanisation and the cold war.

Cheap oil, the automobile, electricity and the mass production revolution created conditions for building cheap houses on cheap land and for filling them with innovative electrical appliances and plastics for all purposes.

Yet, in order to enable widespread ownership, the public sector built the roads, provided mortgage guarantees, unemployment insurance and pensions, while the private sector developed various new forms of consumer credit for housing, cars and appliances.

Labour unions kept salaries growing with productivity, while progressive tax structures funded the welfare state, military procurement and R&D. International stability, trade and investment were enabled by the IMF, the dollar as gold, the General Agreement on Tariffs and Trade and the World Bank. It was a set of bold and imaginative institutional innovations, most of them thanks to John Maynard Keynes, which provided dynamic and solvent demand guiding innovation, investment and expansion.

Altogether it was a positive sum game between business and society – a win-win solution that brought a 'golden age' indeed!

Is there a direction ahead that could play that role with the ICT revolution today? Is there one that fulfils the aspirations of people in developed and developing countries, and is compatible with hard limits on global resources? Yes. That direction is 'green growth', accompanied by full global development.

FOCUS ON INTANGIBLE GROWTH

Green growth is not just about addressing climate change. It is about shifting production and consumption patterns towards intangible goods, materials and energy saving, multiplying the productivity of resources and creating new markets for special materials, renewable energy, really durable products for business models based on rental rather than possession, a huge increase in personal – quality of life – services, and so on. It implies a redefinition of the aspirational 'good life' towards the health of the individual and the environment, imitating the educated elites (as has happened historically).

And the win-win green growth direction also implies full global development. Why? Because that is what would create growing demand for equipment, infrastructure, and engineering, all rede-signed in a green and sustainable direction, while enabling increasing production and innovation for the domestic and export markets in all countries.

Accelerating the already existing shifts in those directions would require a major set of policy innovations, including a radical reform of the tax system to change relative profitability. For instance, instead of salaries, profits and VAT, we might need to tax materials, energy and transactions. Does that sound like a major change? Yes, and it needs to be!

These are times for as much institutional imagination and bold leadership as were displayed to shape the previous technological revolution. Putting patches on the old policies will not do the job. As for finance, the opportunities for profitable innovation would then be innumerable. New models would be needed to fund the green transformation, plus the knowledge intensive enterprises, the new social economy practices, the investment needs of global development and so on. For governments, this means putting 'innovation at the centre of economic growth policy'.

I hope that this way of understanding the task at hand can help to initiate a serious dialogue between innovation economists and macro/finance economists. Once the global economy finds the green pathway for competitiveness and profitability, the measures to avoid short-termism and promote long-term investment would be truly effective. They would be supporting a real economy that is dynamic and innovative. Let us all stop worrying about the supposed 'secular stagnation' due to lack of investment opportunities, and let us unleash the transformative potential of technology by creating the conditions for the next 'golden age'.

Carlota Perez is centennial professor of international development at the London School of Economics; professor of technology and development at the Nurkse Institute, Technological University of Tallinn; and honorary professor at SPRU, University of Sussex. Her book, *Technological Revolutions and Financial Capital: The Dynamics of Bubbles and Golden Ages*, has contributed to the present understanding of the relationship between technical and institutional change, finance and economic development.

NOTES

1. Piketty T. and Saez E. (2010; update of 2003) 'Income Inequality in the United States 1913–1998', *The Quarterly Journal of Economics*, 115 (1): 1–39. Available at http://elsa.berkeley.edu/~saez/#income (accessed 10/03/13).

2. See Perez, C. (2002) 'Technological Revolutions and Financial Capital: The Dynamics of Bubbles and Golden Ages'. Cheltenham: Edward Elgar; Perez, C. (2009) 'The Double Bubble at the Turn of the Centu-

ry: Technological Roots and Structural Implications', *Cambridge Journal of Economics*, 33:4, 779–805; Perez C. (2013a) 'Financial Bubbles, Crises and the Role of Government in Unleashing Golden Ages' in Pyka, A. and Burghof, H.P. (eds.) *Innovation and Finance.* London: Routledge; Perez, C. (2013b) 'Unleashing a Golden Age After the Financial Collapse: Drawing Lessons From History', *Environmental Innovation and Societal Transitions*, 6, 9–23.

WHY WE NEED PUBLIC ENDOWMENTS FOR TRANSFORMATIVE RESEARCH

Arun Majumdar

We routinely use our smartphones without realising the research and development that produced them: the transistor, integrated circuits, wireless communication, the laser and optical communication, the internet, the Unix operating system, and so on. None of these existed during the second world war. But as Mariana Mazzucato has shown in her book, *The Entrepreneurial State*, four decades of post-war research created the foundation for today's products. Can we learn any principles about research and how it should be funded as a result of this example?

Here are some observations:

- **Basic and applied research should not be separated**

    The common myth is that there is basic research and then it hands over to applied research, which then hands over to technology and innovations. That is a myth, to put it lightly. Basic research, which tries to understand 'how nature works', is often inseparable from applied research, which is focused on the question 'can we do something useful with it?' What exists between basic and applied research is not one-way traffic, but rather a feedback loop in which applied research generates questions that stimulate basic research – and the cycle continues.

- **Both basic and applied research take time to mature**

The first paper on the protocols used in today's internet was published by Robert Kahn and Vint Cerf[1] in 1974. These protocols were implemented on the ARPAnet in 1983, nine years later; it took another nine to 10 years of persistent funding and advocacy for this to become the internet. Indeed, it often takes 15 to 20 years for transformative technologies to create new industries. It does not happen over two or three, or even five years. Now we are still exploring the implications of the internet in various things. It takes time to mature. Therefore, persistent, patient funding is very, very important to nurture the science and engineering that needs to happen for innovation.

- **R&D is not a straight line**

R&D happens in very unpredictable ways. While the development of the smartphone may seem obvious to some, its historical path was far from it. The first transistor was a point contact transistor made of germanium, which no one uses today. The idea of a field-effect transistor, the workhorse of the integrated circuit, and silicon as the material of choice, came much later. Did Kahn and Cerf ever think the internet would develop to take on the shape and form it is has today? I seriously doubt it. There is plenty of serendipity involved, and the paths to successful technologies and products contain many twists and turns. Some humility regarding the ability to predict the direct business impact of research is much needed.

- **Failure is important**

Research is a risky business with plenty of failures. But if we do not fail in our attempts to surpass the state-of-the-art and do something new, we will never learn. Progress is often made when some research results violate the conventional wisdom and new understanding and opportunities arise. In fact, that can often be the competitive advantage. There are lots of failures in the research and innovation process. There are lots of skeletons out there in the history of information and communication technologies – and those were, again, opportunities to learn from. When you go in one direction, there are a lot of blind alleys you do not know about. But you have got to go there and find out, and then come back again and figure out a pathway.

THE DIVISION OF LABOUR IN THE INNOVATION PROCESS

Given this reality of how research works and how it creates value, the question then arises of who should bear the cost – public, private or both – and how it should be executed.

I would divide technologies into two kinds, both expressed as techno-economic learning or experience curves, as illustrated in Figure 6.1.

Existing Technologies

Firstly, existing technologies (see Figure 6.1). When research is focused on evolutionary or incremental improvements in order to go down existing learning curves – for example, Moore's Law,[2] which is critically important for economic growth – there is no question that the private sector must bear a large fraction of the cost, since it affects their bottom line. There is the possibility of a public/private partnership, but the industry has to bear a substantial amount of the cost of doing that research.

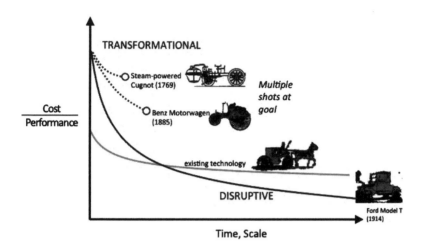

Figure 6.1. Technologies That Lead to Fundamentally New Learning Curves
(*Source:* Author's construction)

Transformative Technologies

However, if we are to conduct research on transformative technologies that create entirely new learning curves or ones where no initial industries exist, then the public sector must invest in a strategic way. There is a 'common good' in this effort, since it is not one or two companies that may benefit from it; rather, it has the potential to create the foundation for entirely new industries, which cannot be exactly predicted *a priori*. Let me explain that by using the example of transportation. In the late 1800s, if someone were to improve the wheel and get a better bearing, and make a faster horse carriage, that is great; that is incremental improvement. But what about the entirely new learning curves that were created at the same time, with the invention of different types of automobiles? At that time the automated car, the horseless carriage, was considered a transformative solution, and there were many of them that failed. Again, those were opportunities to learn from; those were the little circles out there. Many did not go any further because they just did not pan out. But one of them did: the Ford Model T, which became disruptive because it became cheaper and cleaner.

In those cases, it is extremely important that the state creates the environment for this kind of disruptive research to be done, for the innovation to diffuse, and for the private sector to come in later on if it is showing signs of success.

Such cases cannot be market driven, because there is no market to begin with, and – by definition – there will be risk and failure. But for those technologies that succeed, the return on investment to the nation more than compensates for all the failures. The Defense Advanced Research Projects Agency investment in research that led to the internet is a great example of this 'common good'.

Now ARPA-E is doing the same in sustainable energy. As the publicly funded technology matures, if there are early signs of future commercial value, the private sector has to bear some cost through public-private partnerships, where private sector investment is crowded in.

A PUBLIC ENDOWMENT?

In these austere times, how can we ensure that the long-term finance needed for these transformative technologies is available?

Given that many transformative research areas have a long-time horizon (10–20 years), the annual government budget process used today is incompatible with such funding because of all the ups and downs of short-term economic cycles.

Ideally, there should be a large public endowment, perhaps grown over a decade, to create an evergreen fund to invest in strategically important research areas: areas that have the potential to impact everyone – energy and climate, medical and health, etc. This should involve fundamental and applied research, which if properly executed and strategically positioned, will stimulate and crowd in the private sector.

The stability and predictability in funding that such a public endowment would create is critically important in order to recruit the best minds to focus on research in these areas. Kahn and Cerf could not have envisaged what the internet would become.

But perhaps with the backing of long-term, patient funding, we can create the foundation for entirely new industries that we cannot currently even imagine. I believe this endowment would be one of the best gifts that our generation can leave behind for our children and grandchildren.

Arun Majumdar is a professor at Stanford University in the faculty of the department of mechanical engineering and a senior fellow of the Precourt Institute for Energy. He was formerly vice-president for energy at Google. From 2009 to 2012 he served as the first director of the US Advanced Research Projects Agency–Energy (ARPA-E), the country's only agency devoted to transformational energy research and development. He also served as the US acting under-secretary of energy. Previously, he was associate laboratory director for energy and environment at Lawrence Berkeley National Laboratory and a professor of mechanical engineering and materials science and engineering at the University of California, Berkeley.

NOTES

1. Robert Elliot 'Bob' Kahn (born December 23, 1938) is an American electrical engineer, who, along with Vint Cerf, invented the Transmission Control Protocol (TCP) and the Internet Protocol (IP), the fundamental communication protocols at the heart of the Internet.

2. 'Moore's law' is the observation that, over the history of computing hardware, the number of transistors in a dense integrated circuit doubles approximately every two years.

SIX DECADES OF MISSION-ORIENTED FINANCE FOR INDUSTRIALISATION, TECHNICAL CHANGE AND INNOVATION IN BRAZIL

Mariano Laplane

Attempts to anticipate technological breakthroughs that could lead to significant changes in the structure of the economy and give birth to new and dynamic markets are predictably intensified during periods of economic crises or prolonged stagnation. This seems to be the case also in the aftermath of the 2008 financial crisis. Today, public and private agents, in both developed and emerging countries, are involved in the search for 'disruptive technologies' that could fuel economic recovery and long-run growth. The list of potential candidates is constantly increasing. In 2013, a McKinsey Global Institute report identified twelve technologies 'that will transform life, business and the global economy': global internet; automation of knowledge work; the internet of things; cloud technology; advanced robotics; autonomous and near-autonomous vehicles; next-generation genomics; energy storage; 3D printing; advanced materials; advanced oil and gas exploration and recovery; and renewable energy.

Almost simultaneously, a commission appointed by the French government recommended investments in seven technological areas that seemed to offer the best opportunities for France: energy storage; recycling of rare metals; seafloor mining and desalination of seawater; vegetable proteins and vegetable chemistry; personalised medicine; technologies for an ageing population; and big data. Other governments and consultancy firms have prepared their own lists.

Beyond the issue of identifying the most promising areas lies the challenge of designing adequate policies to explore the technological and economic opportunities that might exist. The combination of technological and market risks and the high volume of financial resources involved in exploring new markets inevitably results in the public sector being called upon to take an active part, bearing the risk and the cost of technological development in frontier areas. Policy design must go well beyond the traditional approach of compensating for market failures, since in this case the target is creating new markets. Policy design in this context must take into account that the high risk and cost of the decisions involved in the process of market creation require strong political and public support. Therefore, public funding of risky and very expensive innovation projects demands careful assessment of the potential technological, economic and welfare improvement payoffs, adequate balance between private and public risks and benefits as well as institutional arrangements that allow close monitoring of the projects once they are approved.

SCIENCE, TECHNOLOGY AND INNOVATION POLICY IN BRAZIL

Brazil, as a latecomer industrialised country, has some experience in creating new markets. The process of industrialisation that started in the 1930s involved progressively establishing suppliers of intermediary and final goods and services as well as the institutional arrangements needed to meet local demand for manufactures. To some extent, latecomer industrialisation consists of a long and complex process of creating new markets. Needless to say, in such processes the risks (and uncertainty) involved are sharply mitigated by the fact that over time imports are a source of valuable information about the type and size of existing demand. Furthermore, establishing local supply capacity frequently involves technologies which elsewhere are relatively mature and available. Nevertheless, the complexities of the industrial catching-up process should not be underestimated, since only a few countries – Brazil among them – succeeded in the attempt during the 20th century.

Foreign direct investment was the main source of the technology required to further the more complex stages of the industrialisation process in the 1950s and 1960s. At that time the first steps were taken towards building stronger local scientific capabilities. Public agencies were established to fund the development of infrastructure and human resources needed for scientific research. It was only in the 1970s, when Brazil faced the challenge of establishing new markets for heavy industries and machinery, that the need to organise sectorial innovation systems that effectively integrated local scientific knowledge and technological capabilities became a priority. State-owned enterprises (SOEs) had an important role in organising and operating such systems in steel, telecommunications, energy, oil, inputs for agriculture and other industries. Innovation systems run by SOEs were 'mission-oriented' from the beginning, aiming to develop capabilities combining technology transfer and local development.

THE CASES OF EMBRAPA AND PETROBRAS

Embrapa and Petrobras are two well-known examples of SOEs that led large-scale, mission-oriented innovation programmes. Such programmes were launched when Brazil was facing extreme hard currency constraints due to huge imports of oil and food and when disruptive innovation was needed to remove obstacle to long-term growth. Public funding was the main source of resources driving the programmes. Petrobras succeeded in developing technology for deep-sea oil and gas prospecting and extraction, and has since become a world leader in the field. Emprapa's research programmes allowed Brazil to expand the agricultural frontier and not only to achieve self-sufficiency but also to become leader in tropical agriculture, food production, and exports.

THE CRISIS OF THE 1980s

The foreign debt crisis in the 1980s resulted in severe cuts in the funding available for investment and research in Brazil, and had a heavy cost for the state-run innovation systems. By the end of the decade the process of industrialisation itself was interrupted and high instability and stagnation ensued. A drastic change in policy was introduced in the following decade. During the 1990s, large-scale privatisation of SOEs in manufacturing and public utilities dismantled most of the existing public innovation systems. Trade liberalisation, market deregulation, and a strong influx of foreign direct investment were expected to stimulate the emergence of more innovative behaviour in the private sector and the building of new innovation systems run by private firms exposed to global competition. Except for a few isolated initiatives, industrial policy was abandoned. Following the advice of multilateral institutions, the state's role was restricted to fixing eventual market failures.

By the end of the decade it became evident that the results of the new policy approach were overall disappointing. Private firms had in fact updated their products and increased their efficiency – mostly by importing equipment and technology – but without an equivalent increase in their local innovation capabilities. An attempt was made to foster innovation capabilities by making more funding available for the private sector through policy instruments that mirrored those existing in OECD countries and by passing legislation to protect industrial property rights. This attempt also involved removing institutional barriers that hampered cooperation between private firms and researchers working at public universities and research institutions.

THE FAILURE OF 'SUPPLY-SIDE'-STYLE INNOVATION POLICY

The new policy package came to be characterised in Brazil as 'sup-ply-side'-style innovation policy, as opposed to the mission-orient-ed or 'public demand-led' policies of the previous decades. The role of the public sector was mostly to provide incentives and at best to 'level the playing field', while the private sector was supposed to choose the best opportunities for innovating. The prevailing view was that the public sector should not 'pick the winners' because of the risk of 'moral hazard' and because it could end up 'crowding out' private innovation efforts. Innovation policy from then on aimed exclusively at correcting 'market failures'. In practice, it was restricted to making 'rational private decision-making' possible in situations where externalities and other market failures could be an obstacle.

A few years after the new policy was implemented, some short-comings became evident. In spite of the new package of incentives, the behaviour of the private sector in Brazil regarding innovation did not change significantly. Business demand for the incentives available remained weak. The results of the 'national innovation surveys' revealed that only a relatively small number of firms in manufacturing – either locally owned or subsidiaries of foreign cor-porations – were involved in innovation activities that required strong local capability building. At the same time, Brazilian manu-facturing was lagging behind in the expansion of the more dynamic sectors, and the import of technology-intensive products was rapidly increasing.

THE NEW INDUSTRIAL POLICY

The answer to the above-mentioned shortcomings resulted in new public sector initiatives. Industrial policy was slowly reintroduced from 2004 onwards and strengthened after 2010; industrial policy and science and technology policy became better coordinated. Public procurement was again used to foster innovation in select areas, like health, energy, and defence industries. Research infrastructure was updated and enlarged. The supply-side approach to innovation policy is now progressively combined with the introduction of programmes led by public demand aiming to create new markets.

THE CHALLENGES FOR PUBLIC AGENCIES

Brazil had some successful experiences running large-scale mission-oriented innovation programmes in the past. Large research programmes run by SOEs in agriculture and the oil industry, for instance, resulted in technological breakthroughs that allowed Brazil to become self-sufficient in food and energy, and had a strong impact on the economic structure. Given uncertainty and high costs, public involvement was crucial in every case. Private organisations, firms, and research institutions, from both Brazil and abroad, were 'crowded in' by public initiatives.

The Center for Management and Strategic Studies (CGEE), a private non-profit organisation created in 2001, brought together many people that took part in such large-scale programmes. Nowadays, the core of CGEE activities consists of foresight studies, strategic evaluation, and information and knowledge management. The centre advises government agencies in charge of science and technology policy in Brazil.

CGEE's experience shows that public agencies involved in large-scale mission-oriented innovation programmes need to bridge three different gaps:

- **The knowledge gap**: Being able to anticipate future 'societal and technological challenges' that can result in 'new technological and market opportunities' is not simple. The challenge goes well beyond identifying potential threats, like climate change impacts, or identifying potentially fruitful knowledge areas, like renewable energy. Organising a research programme for 'disruptive innovation' involves a much more detailed definition of the target. The specification of the problem, of the strategy, and of the resources needed takes time and requires previous knowledge that is not always immediately available to public agencies.

- **The coordination gap**: Organising and running large-scale mission-oriented innovation programmes demands a great deal of information gathering, processing, and sharing among government agencies, business, and scientists. Coordinating the actions of groups with heterogeneous interests and mindframes demands special skills and previous experience that are not always available. Public agencies usually have some experience facing such challenges in large defence-related programmes, but not in other areas.

- **The technology management gap**: Efficient assessment and monitoring of mission-oriented innovation programmes requires the ability to use technology management tools such as those needed to assess the degree of maturity of available technologies or the tools used to identify technologies that are critical to the success of a given programme. Private firms operating long-run and complex innovation projects as well as public agencies in charge of defence or space programmes usually have experience in using technology management tools, unlike most public agencies in other areas.

Public agencies running mission-oriented innovation programmes need to bridge the three aforementioned gaps to be successful. The ability to overcome the challenges depends on effective capability building within the agencies involved.

CRITERIA FOR ESTABLISHING MISSION-ORIENTED PROGRAMMES

Basically, four different criteria need to be taken into consideration when assessing competing alternative programmes. The first criterion is the traditional cost and benefit balance in technological, economic, and welfare improvement terms. The second criterion takes technological risk into account and demands an assessment of the degrees of maturity and criticality of the technologies involved. The third criterion deals with market risk and involves assessing the type of institutional arrangements needed to make the innovation result in a new market. This requires assessing issues such as: the need to introduce new regulation, and the need to involve other public and/ or private agents so that the economic and societal payoff of innovation is fully exploited. In the decision-making process for mission-oriented programmes, public agencies must be guided by compared expected costs and benefits, as well as the technological and market risks involved.

THE ENTREPRENEURIAL STATE MUST BE A DEMOCRATIC STATE

Lastly, but also of crucial importance, is the need to assess – beforehand – the degree of public support for the initiatives. Disruptive innovations can be very expensive and can mean channelling huge amounts of public funds towards highly uncertain or risky projects. Thus, unlike the programmes run by SOEs in Brazil in the 1970s, public-demand-led programmes need to be submitted to democratic debate before decisions are made.

Public opinion should be allowed to assess the potential payoff and the burden of risk and rewards taken by society and private sector agents willing to co-invest in the programme.

The role of the state in this context goes well beyond 'de-risking' initiatives to further private innovation decisions. It involves strong entrepreneurial action based on the long-run potential gains for society in the creation of new markets. Citizens must be allowed to express their preferences. Thus, the entrepreneurial state must be a democratic state.

Mariano Laplane is the president of the Center for Strategic Studies and Management, a social organisation affiliated to the

Brazilian Ministry of Science, Technology and Innovation. He is also associate professor at the Institute of Economics of the State University of Campinas, where he heads the graduate study programme. He has an MA in city planning from the University of California, Berkeley, and a PhD in economics from UNICAMP. He is a member of the Mercosur Economic Research Network based in Montevideo.

CHALLENGES AND OPPORTUNITIES FOR A KNOWLEDGE-BASED UK ECONOMY

Vince Cable

My starting point is that our objective in policy must be to create a successful, knowledge-based economy which rests on innovation and a highly skilled labour force. That is what my own job is about.

It is unfashionable but essential to remind people of the real achievements of state-sponsored innovation. An accurate history of the state's role in technological progress is one we urgently needed, and that has now been offered by Mariana Mazzucato's book *The Entrepreneurial State.*[1] It really is important to acknowledge the public investment without which railways, aviation, nuclear power, pharmaceuticals, space exploration, computer science and the internet could never have evolved as quickly or at scale. Today, current moves into green technologies, robotics, personalised medicine, and 'smart cities' are just as reliant on public investment or other support as previous endeavours. As Mazzucato pointed out, Medical Research Council–sponsored projects during the 1970s, which led to the discovery of monoclonal antibodies, are now responsible for around a third of all new drug treatments.

Some dangerous myths have proliferated. You will probably have heard the following Ronald Reagan quote: "The most terrifying words in the English language are: I'm from the government and I'm here to help." It is often used to buttress ideological preferences against state intervention, but Reagan was also the president responsible for the US Small Business Innovation Research programme, which we have sought to emulate in the UK with the Orphan Drug Act, a shot in the arm for the biotech industry; not to mention Star Wars, which has done wonders for technological innovation even if the Evil Empire dissolved without a laser gun being fired in anger.

And that example illustrates the need to also recognise the limits to the role of the state as innovator and entrepreneur. The Soviet Union is no longer with us in large part because an overbearing, centralised state suffocated – rather than encouraged – innovation. Innovation needs a mixed economy: profit-seeking entrepreneurs as well as an entrepreneurial state. And we need to be hard-headed rather than over-romantic about the entrepreneurial state. Private businesses lose their own money; government loses money that has an opportunity cost in poorer public finances and higher tax.

THE COALITION'S RECORD

Our mission is to establish the UK as a leading knowledge economy. But critical as it is to have a healthy, profitable private sector, it will not, on its own, generate large-scale innovation in areas where there are higher risks and wider benefits. That requires a commitment to public investment in science and innovation, albeit with the caveat I have set out above. We need mechanisms to ensure that public investment is properly evaluated for its prospective returns. A new Department for Business, Innovation and Skills report[2] analysed traditional and emerging barriers to innovation in those sectors with dedicated industrial strategies, to better help us understand where public investment can make a difference.

There is much common ground between Mazuccato's position and the one staked out by my team in BIS. We have given considerable thought to the processes through which innovation occurs in practice – which prompted me to launch the Catapult centres early in our administration, funding a practical link between new science and commercial innovation and drawing on the German Fraunhofer model.

Common ground is also evident in our emphasis on planning for the long term, epitomised by the industrial strategy – a partnership with business whose commitments go much further than narrowly 'addressing market failures'. Here it is vital that we look beyond party point-scoring and beyond the time frame of single parliaments, so that business has the confidence to innovate on the back of the technology push we are giving.

This administration has done much in recognition of the role of public funding. In last year's spending round we committed to increasing science capital funding in real terms from £0.6bn in 2012–2013 to £1.1bn in 2015–2016. We are protecting the £4.6bn per annum funding for science and research programmes in cash terms during the current spending review period. We also set a long-term capital budget for science into the next parliament, which will grow in line with inflation to 2020–2021, and we increased the budget of Innovate UK (formerly the Technology Strategy Board) in the last spending round by £185m for 2015–2016, taking it to over £500m.

WHY WE NEED TO DO MORE

But I now want to advance the economic argument, in order to make the case that we need to do more. And this is why:

My first premise is that science and innovation are critical to economic growth and the long-term development of our economy. Of the productivity growth that took place in the UK between 2000 and 2008, one third (32 per cent) was attributable to changes in technology resulting from science and innovation.[3] Innovative firms are also more resilient and more likely to export, though there is a serious export challenge facing the UK.[4]

Innovation is a critical driver of productivity, an area in which the UK has what some in the Bank of England have referred to as a 'puzzle', but which I would call a serious imbalance. UK productivity is around 16 per cent off its pre-crisis trend,[5] and the Office for Budget Responsibility sees the outlook for productivity growth as the key uncertainty for the economy. But fascination with the puzzle of Britain's weak productivity risks obscuring a broader trend of structurally and comparatively lower productivity than our competitors, and this is where the importance of innovation is clear. Around two thirds of our productivity lag with the US can be attributed to weaker innovation and ways of working.

Looking across countries and across sectors, firms that persistently invest in R&D have higher productivity – 13 per cent higher than those with no R&D spending and nine per cent more than firms who occasionally invest in R&D.[6]

Innovating firms are more resilient and export more. Innovation also underpins business resilience, and finally, innovation plays an important role in our export ambitions. SMEs that have a track record of innovation are more likely to export, more likely to export successfully, and more likely to generate growth from exporting than non-innovating firms.[7]

BRITAIN INVESTS LESS IN R&D
THAN ITS COMPETITORS

The second premise is that if we consistently invest less in our science and innovation capabilities than our competitors, we cannot expect to sustain the UK as a world leader in knowledge-based activity.

The UK research base continues to produce a large output for its moderate size, with a sustained track record of high-quality research. With a mere four per cent of the world's researchers, we account for six per cent of world articles, 12 per cent of citations (a key measure of research excellence) and 16 per cent of the most highly cited articles.[8]

But the UK's total investment in R&D – both public and private – has been relatively static, at around 1.8 per cent of GDP since the early 1990s and standing at 1.7 per cent of GDP in 2012, the last year for which we have data.[9]

In contrast, the US alone spends around £250bn (2.8 per cent of GDP) on R&D per annum. China increased its R&D by 28 per cent in 2009 and 15 per cent in 2010, to roughly £125bn (1.8 per cent of GDP), and South Korea doubled its expenditure between 2003 and 2011 to around £35bn (four per cent of GDP). France and Germany have consistently invested substantially more than two per cent of their GDP in R&D, with aspirations to increase this to three per cent or more.

PUBLIC SECTOR SUPPORT FOR INNOVATION LAGS BEHIND OTHER COUNTRIES

Public sector support for innovation is harder to compare, but such data as exists suggests that UK funding is at the lower end of the scale. If we look at innovation support specifically (as opposed to wider research), as a share of GDP, Finland spends almost 10 times as much per capita on TEKES (its Innovate UK equivalent) than we do.[10] We so far invest in our Catapults less than one tenth of what Germany spends on its Fraunhofer Institutes and of what France has committed to its equivalent, the Centre National de la recherche scientifique (CNRS) (£135m v £1.6bn and £2bn), though this is from a standing start three years ago and will increase.

In a globally competitive environment, this comparatively weak performance risks jeopardising the breadth and depth of science and innovation excellence required to underpin our industrial success and the capacity of our firms to absorb and apply new knowledge and ideas.

DIRECT PUBLIC INVESTMENTS AS A SOLUTION

My third premise, building on the second, is that alongside tax incentives for R&D, public investment is also part of the solution to our chronic private sector underinvestment. Business expenditure on R&D grew eight per cent in real terms between 2001 and 2012,[11] but – as a share of total output – it has flatlined since 2007 at around 1.1 per cent. It remains to be seen how far tax credits alleviate that deficiency, but there is still a case for strong public investment. Rather than 'crowding out', the literature offers strong evidence that public investment in science and innovation 'crowds in' private investment.

There is potential for public investment to drive virtuous circles of private investment and innovation, as quality of research attracts international talent which in turn attracts global companies – all of which results in further advances both in new knowledge and exploitation.

AND IT WORKS

The fourth premise is that what we have done so far has worked. For example, we know that innovation support increases firms' survival probability by around three per cent over a decade.[12] A second report[13] synthesised the evidence on the returns to government investment in science and innovation; it confirmed that social returns are significant – normally two or three times greater than their private benefits, and persisting long into the future. Innovate UK investment to support business-led innovation has generated a return to the economy of between £3 and £9 of additional value (gross value added) for each £1 of public money invested.

At these rates, investment in UK science and innovation will pay for itself many times over.

WHAT DOUBLING PUBLIC INVESTMENT WOULD MEAN

A doubling of innovation spend is what a serious commitment to innovation means. It was this kind of commitment in the aerospace sector, via the Aerospace Growth Partnership, that retrieved a sector at risk of drifting away.

The annual Innovate UK core budget is approximately 0.03 per cent of GDP, or £500m. Doubling annual innovation spend could bring its resources closer to £1bn. It would enable the Catapult network to be deepened and widened, and to leverage in greater private funding. It would also enable Innovate UK to fund more of the strong applications it receives. A further £500m of public investment could mean at least £1bn more of innovation spend every year across the UK. This would close some of the gap on our competitors, moving us closer towards the important figure of 2.9 per cent of GDP spend as being the indicative level necessary for the UK's future economic success.

CONCLUSION

In sum, the case for public support for science and innovation is, to me, unequivocal. Science and innovation require patience, and grants have the capacity to promote long-term support. Mazuccato has illustrated how venture capital arrived only 20 years after key public investments were made in biotech, nanotech, and the technologies underpinning the internet. For a single field of medicine, the Wellcome Trust[14] assumes the lag between public and charitable R&D spending on cardiovascular research and measurable health gains to be 17 years.

Investments made today are for the sake of breakthroughs whose effects will be felt by the next generation or the one after that. We need long-term planning and commitment, and the need to create certainty. I want there to be no doubt in the minds of overseas investors, of world-class scientists, of budding entrepreneurs, that the UK is the best place in the world for them to invest, research, collaborate, and start a business.

Vince Cable is UK secretary of state for business, innovation and skills and MP for Twickenham. He studied natural science

and economics at Cambridge University, followed by a PhD at Glasgow University. He served in the Liberal Democrat shadow cabinet as spokesman on trade and industry (1999–2003), shadow chancellor (2003–2010), and deputy leader of the Liberal Democrats (2006–2010). Cable worked as Treasury finance officer for the Kenyan government in the 1960s as well as in a range of senior academic, economic and foreign policy roles before becoming Shell International's chief economist in 1995.

NOTES

1. Mazzucato, M. (2013) *The Entrepreneurial State: Debunking the Public Vs. Private Myth in Risk and Innovation.* London: Anthem Press.

2. Technopolis (2014) *The Case for Public Support of Innovation At the Sector, Technology and Challenge Area Levels.* Available at https://www.gov.uk/government/uploads/system/uploads/attachment_data/file/334369/BIS_14_852_The_Case_for_Public_Support_of_Innovation.pdf (accessed on 16/1/2015).

3. Goodridge, Haskel and Wallis (2012) *UK Innovation Index: Productivity and Growth in UK Industries*, Nesta Working Paper no. 12/09. Available at www.nesta.org.uk/wp12-09 (accessed on 16/1/2015).

4. Birkbeck (2014) *Innovation, Skills and Performance in the Downturn.* Available at https://www.gov.uk/government/uploads/system/uploads/attachment_data/file/287901/bis-14-652-innovation-skills-and-performance-in-the-downturn.pdf (accessed on 16/1/2015); Enterprise Research Centre (2014) *Growing Global – Moving up the Exporting Ladder.* Insight Paper. June 2014. Available at http://enterpriseresearch.ac.uk/wp-content/uploads/2014/06/ERC-Insight-Conf-2014-Innov.pdf (accessed on 16/1/2015).

5. Office for National Statistics (2014). *International Comparisons of Productivity – First Estimates, 2013.* Available at http://www.ons.gov.uk/ons/rel/icp/international-comparisons-of-productivity/2013---first-estimates/stb-icp1014.html (accessed on 16/1/2015).

6. Lööf et al (2012) 'R&D Strategy and Firm Performance: What is the Long-Run Impact of Persistent R&D?' in *Innovation & Growth: From*

R&D Strategies of Innovating Firms to Economy-Wide Technological Change. Oxford University Press.

7. Love and Roper (2013) *SME Innovation, Exporting and Growth: A review of Existing Evidence*. Enterprise Research Centre. White Paper Number 5. Available at http://enterpriseresearch.ac.uk/wp-content/uploads/2013/12/ERC-White-Paper-No_5-Innovation-final.pdf (accessed on 16/1/2015).

8. Elsevier (2013) *International Comparative Performance of the UK Research Base – 2013*. Available at https://www.gov.uk/government/uploads/system/uploads/attachment_data/file/263729/bis-13-1297-international-comparative-performance-of-the-UK-research-base-2013.pdf (accessed on 16/1/2015).

9. Office for National Statistics (2014) *Gross Domestic Expenditure on Research and Development, 2012*. Available at http://www.ons.gov.uk/ons/rel/rdit1/gross-domestic-expenditure-on-research-and-development/2012/index.html (accessed on 16/1/2015).

10. Allas, T. (2014) *Insights from International Benchmarking of the UK Science and Innovation System*, BIS Analysis Paper No. 3, Department for Business, Innovation and Skills. Available at https://www.gov.uk/government/publications/science-and-innovation-system-international-benchmarking (accessed on 16/1/2015).

11. In 2013, total expenditure on R&D performed in UK businesses, in constant prices, increased by six per cent compared with 2012. Office for National Statistics (2014) *Business Enterprise Research and Development, 2013*. Available at http://www.ons.gov.uk/ons/dcp171778_385959.pdf (accessed on 16/1/2015).

12. Specifically, firms which receive public support for innovation are 2.7 per cent more likely to survive for eight years than firms which innovate but without public support. Enterprise Research Centre (2014) *Innovation, Innovation Strategy and Survival*. Research Paper no. 17. Available at http://enterpriseresearch.ac.uk/publications/innovation-innovation-strategy-survival/ (accessed on 16/1/2015).

13. Frontier Economics (2014) *Rates of Return to Investment in Science and Innovation*. Available at https://www.gov.uk/government/uploads/system/uploads/attachment_data/file/333006/bis-14-990-rates-of-return-to-investment-in-science-and-innovation-revised-final-report.pdf (accessed on 16/1/2015).

14. Wellcome (2008) *Medical Research: What's It Worth? Estimating the Economic Benefits from Medical Research in the UK*. Available at http://www.wellcome.ac.uk/stellent/groups/corporatesite/@sitestudio objects/documents/web_document/wtx052110.pdf (accessed on 16/1/ 2015).

WHY A FUNDAMENTAL SHIFT IN INNOVATION POLICY IS NEEDED

Tera Allas

Innovation is a big deal: the continued prosperity of knowledge-based economies depends on it.[1] However, innovation outcomes are determined by a web of complementary interactions, and therefore require systemic solutions. The public sector is often poorly equipped to deal with this complexity. Yet, just by existing, governments play a major role – and need to get better at it. A key part of this is transforming cost-benefit frameworks to take account of the real-world behaviour of economic agents and innovation systems. On this foundation, governments can set up truly strategic innovation interventions that match world's best practice and make a material difference.

ENHANCING INNOVATION REQUIRES SYSTEMIC SOLUTIONS

Innovation is at the heart of economic growth and prosperity. For example, it is estimated that around 50 per cent of labour productivity growth in the UK between 2000 and 2008 was associated with innovation[2] (Figure 9.1). Moreover, most developed economies' performance relies disproportionately on sectors that are research- and innovation-intensive.[3]

However, taking the UK as a case study, our innovation performance is decidedly mediocre. Compared to an EU27 average of 53 per cent, only 44 per cent of UK businesses record innovation activity (Figure 9.2). New-to-market innovations account for only seven per cent of UK firms' turnover – half that of the average for all EU countries.[4]

There is no one cause for this underperformance: innovation outcomes are the result of complex and interconnected systems that incorporate investment, human capital, institutional structures, mar-

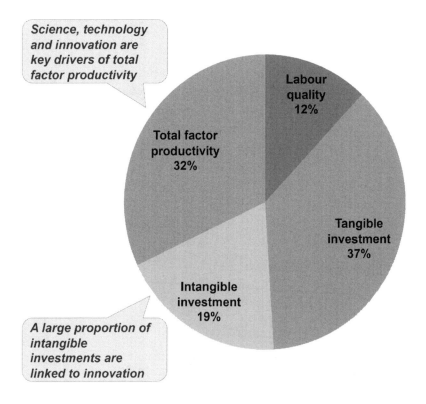

Figure 9.1. Sources of Growth in UK Labour Productivity 2000–2008 (estimates of drivers of labour productivity are volatile, so should be taken as indicative only) (*Source:* NESTA [2012], *op. cit*)

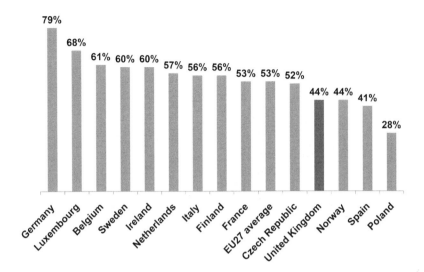

Figure 9.2. Percentage of All Enterprises Engaging in Innovation Activity 2008–2010 (*Source:* Eurostat [2013], *Proportion of Innovative Enterprises 2008–10*, European Commission Eurostat Innovation Statistics, available at http://epp.eurostat.ec.europa.eu/statistics_explained/index.php/Innovation_statistics, accessed on 12/10/2014)

ket and policy incentives, and the broader business and regulatory environment.[5] Therefore, in order to enhance prospects for the future, it is necessary to identify and apply systemic solutions.

GOVERNMENTS PLAY A MAJOR ROLE, WHETHER THEY LIKE IT OR NOT

It could be argued that it is precisely this kind of complex system that the public sector is poor at dealing with, and that government policy should be confined to a limited set of circumstances where there are clear market failures such as public goods or natural monopolies. However, such a stance is unrealistic and misleading, for three reasons:

- Just by existing, governments have a major impact on innovation.
- In practice, governments already intervene in a myriad of ways.
- Innovation systems exhibit increasing returns – so small may not be beautiful (see next section).

The first two points here can be illustrated by looking at the four levels at which government policy shapes the factors that make successful innovation either more or less likely:

- At the broadest level, government sets the taxation and corporate governance framework, planning regime and other regulations – such as antitrust and intellectual property protection – that govern private sector firms' behaviour and incentives.
- Governments are major economic actors in their own right. For example, in the UK, in 2012–2013, government expenditure accounted for 43 per cent of GDP.[6] The way it goes about procurement and delivery therefore affects the system as a whole.
- Many of the critical inputs into the innovation system – such as education and skills, scientific research and infrastructure – are partly or even predominantly funded (and often delivered) by the government.
- A vast array of policies – including standards, regional and local policy, export promotion, enterprise schemes and, indeed, innovation support[7] – are targeted at enhancing economic growth, and as such directly impact on innovation.

The real question, then, is not whether, but how governments should drive innovation. Are the specific initiatives at efficient scale? Do they fully exploit increasing returns[8] such as critical mass effects and cluster benefits? Why is the picture so fragmented?

COST-BENEFIT FRAMEWORKS NEED TO REFLECT EMPIRICAL REALITY

There is one particularly pervasive factor that contributes to fragmentation: the cost-benefit framework that underpins decisions about government interventions.[9] While the guidance itself[10] allows for system dynamics and agents with bounded rationality, the way it is implemented frequently underplays these real-life complexities.[11] Its insistence on a 'do nothing' option anchors decision-makers to prefer small-scale interventions (Figure 9.3), which are destined to have limited impact in the presence of increasing returns.[12]

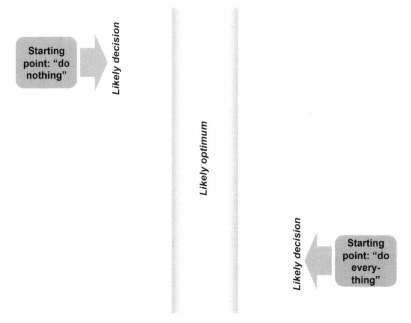

Figure 9.3. The Anchoring Effect of the 'Do Nothing' Default Assumption (*Source*: Author's construction)

LEADING ACADEMICS AND PRACTITIONERS
POINT THE WAY FORWARD

The panel discussion at the MOFI conference in London in July 2014 reflected the challenging set of issues at play. Encouragingly, however, there were a number of common themes that emerged:

- **Directionality:** For spheres of innovation that involve whole systems, such as energy, it is instrumental that someone clearly articulates the long-term challenges (or missions) and harnesses policy to deliver the necessary experiments and solutions.
- **Scale over scope:** Because government resources to support innovation are finite, it is more likely that they have impact if there is sustained focus on a handful of critical long-term challenges (or missions), rather than spreading activity too thinly.
- **Public engagement:** Policymakers and agencies must not take for granted the legitimacy of government innovation interventions or the applications of novel technology that arise: active engagement with the public is necessary and often enhances the success of interventions.
- **Professional execution:** Effective implementation of innovation policies requires hard-nosed programme management, active portfolio evolution (including stopping initiatives that are not delivering), and reaching out to all actors in the market to build the right networks for success.
- **Broad integration:** Innovation interventions are emphatically not just about the money: the right leadership, skills, networks, infrastructure, market opportunities, and scale-up capabilities all need to come together for innovations to make a real difference. [13]

A FUNDAMENTAL SHIFT IN GOVERNMENTS' APPROACH IS REQUIRED

Given the fundamental importance of innovation to prosperity and the resources dedicated by governments to supporting it, we cannot afford a mediocre effort.

Governments need to think big and stop or scale up immaterial activities; prioritise and focus to ensure clear directionality; take an end-to-end perspective and coordinate across boundaries; and build the structures and capabilities to deliver truly strategic interventions.

Tera Allas is former director general (strategic advice, science and innovation leadership) at the UK Department for Business, Innovation and Skills and former deputy head of the government Economic Service. She serves as a strategic and economic advisor to a number of governmental, business and third sector organisations internationally, and previously held chief economist positions at the UK Department for Transport and the Department of Energy and Climate Change. Prior to this, she worked for 10 years as a management consultant at McKinsey & Company, focusing on corporate and business unit strategy and corporate finance. She holds an MSc in technology and industrial economics (with distinction) from Helsinki University of Technology and an MBA (with distinction) from INSEAD, France.

NOTES

1. This note is based on the conference session 'Innovation in the Public Sector: Market-failure Fixing vs. Mission-Oriented Policies'. It draws on the policy paper written for the conference (available at http://missionorientedfinance.com/wp-content/uploads/2014/07/MOFI-2014-PB-03-Allas.pdf) as well as panel members' presentations and discussion on the day. I would like to thank the panellists, Iain Gray, Mariano Laplane

and Cheryl Martin, and the discussant, Dan Breznitz, for their insights which have contributed to this note.

2. NESTA. (2012) *UK Innovation Index: Productivity and Growth in UK Industries*, NESTA Working Paper 12/09, available at http://www. nesta.org.uk/sites/default/files/uk_innovation_index_productivity_and_ growth_in_uk_industries.pdf; accessed on 12/10/2014.

3. See, for example, page 10, Allas, T. (2014) *Insights from International Benchmarking of the UK Science and Innovation System*, BIS Analysis Paper No. 3, Department for Business, Innovation and Skills, available at https://www.gov.uk/government/publications/science-and-innovation-system-international-benchmarking; accessed on 12/10/2014.

4. European Commission. (2014) *Innovation Union Scoreboard*, available at http://ec.europa.eu/enterprise/policies/innovation/files/ius/ius-2014_en.pdf; Accessed on 12/10/2014.

5. Allas, T. (2014) *Insights from International Benchmarking of the UK Science and Innovation System*, Department for Business, Innovation and Skills, available at https://www.gov.uk/government/publications/ science-and-innovation-system-international-benchmarking; accessed on 12/10/2014; Freeman, Chris. (1995) 'The "National System of Innovation" in Historical Perspective', *Cambridge Journal of Economics 1995*, 19, 5–24, available at http://www.globelicsacademy.org/2011_pdf/Freeman %20NSI%20historial%20perspective.pdf; accessed on 12/10/2014.

6. This has increased from a recent low of around 36 per cent in 1999–2000; the current government projects this figure to come down to around 38 per cent in 2018–2019. See HM Treasury. (2014) *Statistical Bulletin: Public Spending Statistics February 2014*, available at https:// www.gov.uk/government/uploads/system/uploads/attachment_data/file/ 285632/PSS_February_2014.pdf; accessed on 12/10/2014.

7. A comprehensive typology of innovation policy measures can be found in Table 1 in MIoIR. (2013*) Compendium of Evidence on Innovation Policy – 20_Impacts of Innovation Policy: Synthesis and Conclusion*, Manchester Institute of Innovation Research and NESTA, available at http:// www.innovation-policy.org.uk/share/20_Impacts%20of%20Innovation %20Policy%20Synthesis%20and%20Conclusion_linked.pdf; accessed on 12/10/2014.

8. Increasing returns occur when the ratio of outputs to inputs increases as more inputs are deployed; it is in direct contrast to diminishing returns, the standard assumption in conventional economics. The terminol-

ogy is often applied to economic returns, implying that the rate of return on an investment increases with size. This can be due to, for example, economies of scale or network effects. Increasing returns are particularly prevalent for knowledge-based products, services, firms, markets and economies. See Arthur, W. B. (1994) *Increasing Returns and Path Dependence in the Economy. Economics, Cognition, and Society.* Ann Arbor: University of Michigan Press.

9. Mazzucato, M. (2013) *The Entrepreneurial State: Debunking the Public Vs. Private Myth in Risk and Innovation.* London: Anthem Press.

10. HM Treasury. (2011) *The Green Book: Appraisal and Evaluation in Central Government, Treasury Guidance*, HM Treasury, available at https://www.gov.uk/government/publications/the-green-book-appraisal-and-evaluation-in-central-governent; accessed on 12/10/2014.

11. For a fuller discussion, see the longer policy paper 'Innovation and the Public Sector: From Static and Subscale to Dynamic and Bold' located at http://missionorientedfinance.com/resources/.

12. For a simple description on why increasing returns alter the optimal portfolio composition, see Allas, T. (2014b) *The Economic Argument for "Picking Winners" in the Presence of Increasing Returns*, available at http://www.scribd.com/doc/228964407/The-Economic-Argument-for-Picking-Winners-in-the-Presence-of-Increasing-Returns; accessed on 12/10/2014.

13. See also a longer version of this paper at http://missionoriented finance.com/wp-content/uploads/2014/07/MOFI-2014-PB-03-Allas.pdf; accessed on 12/10/2014.

Part III

Learning from Success and Failure

DEVELOPMENT, UNCERTAINTY AND THE ROLE OF STATE INVESTMENT BANKS

Luciano Coutinho, João Carlos Ferraz and Felipe Silveira Marques

The aims of this chapter are twofold: first, to define the concept of uncertainty in relation to specific challenges that arise during the process of economic development; second, to explain the role that development banks – or state investment banks (SIBs) – can play towards mitigating different types and sources of uncertainty.

DEVELOPMENT AND UNCERTAINTY

According to Chris Freeman's classical typology, development projects may face four sources of uncertainty: the complexity of the project; the time frame of investment; the prevailing economic conditions; and lastly, political and policy priorities in the allocation of resources.[1]

By development projects, we mean projects whose objective is to transform the economy at local, regional, or national level. Of special importance are transformative infrastructure projects and projects aiming at disruptive innovations.[2]

The complexity of development projects has three different dimensions: the complexities of the project's preparation – involving as it might a large number of different actors and instruments, especially financial ones;[3] the potential positive and negative externalities to be generated, especially environmentally and socially; and the nature of technologies involved in physical investments. The latter deserves further exploration.

TECHNICAL PROGRESS IS ALWAYS UNCERTAIN

Uncertainty is very much embedded in technical progress. First, the technical base of any specific project is not 'frozen', but rather frequently in flux as a result of automation, scale economics or process innovations. Moreover – and this is increasingly the case – general purpose technologies such as ICTs and new materials are being constantly applied to all types of investment, with consequences for the efficiency and quality of services to be rendered by these projects.

Second, contemporary innovations that have the potential to bring about disruptive change are increasingly dependent on advanced scientific knowledge and on the convergence of different technologies. In others words, innovation is nowadays more complex and interdisciplinary. As a result, innovations depend on cooperation between firms, scientific institutions and technology labs, and therefore encompass a wide variety of capabilities – the so-called 'systems of innovation' – at national, regional, or local level.[4]

Stand-alone research labs within a particular firm simply do not have the means to accumulate all the necessary competences for a given innovation challenge. Thus, the uncertainties surrounding innovation arise not only because of the pursuit of something that does not yet exist, but also because of the need for innovators – firms or research institutions – to bring together partners that have complementary technological capabilities and who can therefore move towards a 'convergent process of building up innovation'.

THE PROBLEM OF TIME SCALES

A second source of uncertainty has to do with the time dimension of investments. Uncertainty particularly affects investments with long maturation processes, especially in a world dominated by short-termism in capital markets.[5] Time matters because it is directly related to investors having to lock up their liabilities with corresponding expectations over future rates of return. The problem is that innovations, especially those of a disruptive nature, may require long time frames before becoming market successes. What is more, success is not guaranteed and investments are constantly subject to dead ends and/or detours, demanding changes in direction that are both costly and time-consuming.

UNCERTAINTIES IN THE ECONOMY AND POLITICS

A third source of uncertainty arises because of prevailing economic conditions, especially long-term macroeconomic stability. Predicting the rules of the game for investment and the level and volatility of long-term interest rates depends directly on the propensity of investors to take risks and allocate long-term capital to specific projects. On top of that come volatile exchange rates, especially where projects involve currency mismatches (for example, costs vs. revenues; assets vs. liabilities).

Finally, it is important to highlight the uncertainties surrounding the political processes that determine priorities for resource allocation. In all countries – more so in democratic ones – governments have a public mandate to pursue a given set of priorities for resource allocation and budget management. However, politicians' time frames may well clash with investment time frames (this is why having public consensus on long-term priorities can mitigate tensions and uncertainties between democratic cycles and the maturation process of long-term investments).

These four sources of uncertainty must be addressed because they can constitute a serious challenge to sustainable economic development in any society.

WHAT DEVELOPMENT BANKS CAN DO

Development banks/SIBs are one of the pillars of resilient financial ecosystems, as they patiently contribute to fostering dynamic economies capable of effectively tackling local and global challenges.[6] Their mission and mandate support development across a wide array of economic activities. Development banks are also relevant for countries at all stages of development – at times of stability as well as of crisis.[7] They are essential in providing support for development strategies, having had an extensive history in long-term financing. There are particular development challenges associated with nascent economic activities and new forms of production and consumption. It is in these sorts of contexts that development banks can foster markets by making strategic public investments in radical innovations, infrastructure, climate change mitigation, and environmental protection.

This chapter proposes that development banks can play an effective role in mitigating the uncertainties inherent in development projects. There are four ways they can do this:

- In order to finance long-term investments, development banks can offer a wide array of instruments of debt or equity suitable for the different stages of innovation and infrastructure projects. These include credit lines with special conditions, grants, credit enhancement mechanisms, direct investment, seed and venture capital or equity funds.
- Development banks can support and foster coordination between relevant actors.
- Being 'mission-oriented' institutions, they have the necessary patience, as they possess an adequate and long-asset and liability base. At the Brazilian National Development Bank the

outstanding credit stock averages 10 years, and most of the bank's liabilities carry much longer durations.
- As a state institution, a development bank participates in the design and support of government policy and can contribute to the longevity of public priorities.

Of course, development banks are a necessary – but not in themselves a sufficient – condition for successful long-term investment in risk-intensive ventures. Societies also need an effective science and technology infrastructure, together with entrepreneurs willing to take chances in the classical Schumpeterian sense. In addition, they need a risk-prone financial industry willing to engage in long-term finance. This is crucial, as the investment frontier may be vast and beyond the means of a sole institution.

THE ROLE OF BNDES

In Brazil, the national development bank, BNDES, has considerable experience in fostering risk-intensive investments. BNDES is the main provider of long-term financing in Brazil, holding two out of three of its bank loans over five years, assets of around $350bn, and disbursing around $80bn per year in total.

BNDES's expenditure on innovation alone currently stands at around $3.5bn, having grown substantially in recent years. The green economy receives around $10bn per year. Financing for infrastructure projects reached $25bn in 2013, and is on the rise. BNDES is quite active in capital markets, both through its portfolio of direct investments and through 35 different funds worth $45bn. Such direct exposure to risk is rewarding: 38 per cent of BNDES's net income between 2007 and 2013 came from BNDESPAR, its investment bank subsidiary.

But to grow in the way BNDES has done in the last few years requires some essential prerequisites: a government's political priorities must be made explicit and enforced; corporate priorities must be aligned to these priorities; and a minimum critical mass of entrepreneurs and research capabilities must exist, in a constant search for strategic opportunities.

An interesting success story, very much within the framework of smart and inclusive growth, is PAISS, a programme to boost second generation, biotech-based ethanol.

Case Study – The PAISS Initiative

The PAISS initiative was based on a strategic vision for Brazil's sugarcane sector: in order to overcome the structural limitations to productivity growth, a change in technological trajectories was required. This would require long-term, risk-intensive investment. So a call for innovation proposals was launched in 2011, with an initial budget of $500m.

After a competitive process, in which 57 companies participated (alone or in partnership with others, together with research institutions), 25 proposals were selected. The initial budget was tripled to $1.5bn and all contracts have now been signed with BNDES and the Brazilian innovation agency, FINEP. PAISS selected GranBio, which operates the southern hemisphere's first commercial-scale plant for second-generation ethanol. The factory, with a production capacity of 82m litres, has been operational since September 2014 in the Brazilian north-east state of Alagoas. It produces biofuel from sugarcane straw and bagasse, the raw material that until then had been discarded or burned in the field.

Building institutions capable of addressing uncertainties is an important task for countries wanting to achieve smart and inclusive growth. Thus, the concluding argument of this chapter is straightforward: institutions that are development-oriented, competent, effective and ethical, and which serve the public interest, can decisively contribute to mitigating the uncertainties surrounding development projects, especially those involving innovation-intensive, smart and inclusive growth.

Luciano Coutinho is president of the Brazilian Development Bank BNDES. He is a specialist in competition law, international trade, and macroeconomic and market forecasting, and winner of the Brazilian-American Chamber of Commerce's Person of the Year 2013 award for his outstanding work in forging closer ties between the two countries.

João Carlos Ferraz is managing director of the BNDES and an economist, specialising in comparative development, industrial economics and public policies. He is currently on leave from his positions as professor of economics at the Economics Institute of the Federal University of Rio de Janeiro and senior economist at the United Nation's Economic Commission for Latin America and the Caribbean.

Felipe Silveira Marques is assistant to the BNDES president and an economist, specialised in the economics of information and communication technologies, holding a PhD from the Economics Institute of the Federal University of Rio de Janeiro.

NOTES

1. Freeman (1982) highlighted technical, market, and general business uncertainties. In Freeman and Soete (1997), they revised the typology to technological, commercial, and organisational uncertainties. See Freeman, C. (1982) *The Economics of Industrial Innovation*, 2nd ed., MIT Press, Cambridge, MA; and Freeman, C., and Soete, L. (1997) *The Economics of Industrial Innovation*, Pinter, London.

2. Perez (2002, p. 31) defined disruptive or radical innovations as improvements that will stretch the life cycle of established technologies or reduce the cost of peripheral activities. They involve change in technological trajectories (Dosi, 1982). See Perez, C. (2002) *Technological Revolutions and Financial Capital: The Dynamics of Bubbles and Golden Ages*, Edward Elgar, Cheltenham; and Dosi, G. (1982) 'Technological Paradigms and Technological Trajectories: A Suggested Interpretation of the Determi-

nants and Directions of Technical Change', *Research Policy,* 11(3), 147–62.

3. CPI (2013) illustrated this point by mapping relevant actors and instruments in 'climate-specific finance', referring specifically to capital flows targeting low-carbon and climate-resilient development with direct or indirect greenhouse gas mitigation or adaptation objectives/outcomes. See CPI (2013) *The Global Landscape of Climate Finance 2013*, available at http://climatepolicyinitiative.org/publication/global-landscape-of-climate-finance-2013/, accessed on 12/10/2014.

4. See, among others, Freeman, C. (1987) *Technology Policy and Economic Performance: Lessons from Japan*, Pinter, London; Lundvall, B.A. (1992) *National Systems of Innovation: Towards a Theory of Innovation and Interactive Learning*, Pinter, London; Nelson, R. (ed.) (1993). *National Innovation Systems: A Comparative Analysis*, Oxford University Press, London; Cassiolato, J.E.; Lastres, H. M.; Maciel, M. (eds.) (2003) *Systems of Innovation and Development*, Edward Elgar, Cheltenham; Pietrobelli, C.; Rabellotti, R. (eds.) (2007) *Upgrading to Compete: SMEs, Clusters and Value Chains in Latin America*, Harvard University Press, Cambridge, MA.

5. Haldane, A.; Davies, R. (2011) 'The Short Long', Speech at the *29th Société Universitaire Européene de Recherches Financières Colloquium: New Paradigms in Money and Finance?*, Brussels, May 2011; Lazonick, W. (2013) 'The Financialization of the U.S. Corporation: What Has Been Lost, and How It Can Be Regained', *Seattle University Law Review,* 36, 857–909.

6. Coutinho, L. (2014) 'Development Banks Good in Crises, Even Better All Other Times', *FT Alphaville Blog*, Mission Finance series, 22/04/14.

7. Ferraz, J. C., Além, A. C. and Madeira, R. F. (2013) 'A contribuição dos bancos de desenvolvimento para o financiamento de longo prazo', *Revista do BNDES,* 40, 5–42.

FINANCING ENERGY INNOVATION: THE CASE OF ARPA-E

Cheryl Martin

The Advanced Research Projects Agency–Energy (ARPA-E) within the US Department of Energy catalyses high-potential, high-impact energy technologies that are too new for private sector investment or traditional government R&D funding. The aim is to explore the uncharted territories of energy technology and to accelerate the pace of innovation. With a rigorous programme design, competitive project selections, and hands-on engagement, it ensures thoughtful expenditures while empowering the US's energy researchers with funding, technical assistance, and market awareness.

The US Congress established ARPA-E in 2007, following a recommendation by the National Academies in their *Rising above the Gathering Storm* report on retaining US leadership in science and engineering. As of August 2014, ARPA-E has funded 380 projects with over $900m. Over one third of this funding has gone to small business; one third has gone to universities; 20 per cent to large businesses; and the remaining funding has gone to national laboratories and non-profit organisations.

THE ARPA-E STRUCTURE

ARPA-E has a unique, nimble, and adaptive structure modelled on the successful Defense Advanced Research Projects Agency, which is responsible for numerous innovations including stealth technology, GPS, and the foundations of the internet. The core of the model is the team, particularly the programme directors and technology-to-market advisers.

Our programme directors provide awardees with technical guidance that combines scientific expertise and real-world experience, while our technology-to-market advisers supply critical business insight and strategies to move technologies towards the market. Both the programme directors and technology-to-market advisers serve limited, three-to-four-year terms, which instils a sense of urgency to succeed and regularly provides a fresh perspective on technologies and market conditions.

Programme development at ARPA-E is primarily about identifying technology gaps where high-impact, high-potential investment could lead to entirely new ways to generate, store, and use energy. We are concerned with framing the challenges of energy in new ways, inviting new eyes, and novel ideas to the table. We look across the entire spectrum of the energy sector for ideas and connections, as it is very dynamic. Think of what was 'known' in energy just five years ago – some of those truths are very different now, and will change and evolve as we move into the future.

That is why ARPA-E is an agency devoted to creating options. It is the 'optionality agency' of energy; therefore, we work across the entire spectrum of energy, from carbon capture to fuel cells, from hardware and software to route the electric grid to energy storage at grid scale, from low-cost utilisation of more of the sun's rays for energy production to conformable gas tanks for natural-gas vehicles. We know that the path of innovation is discontinuous and unpredictable and, to be effective, you have to do more than just set out objectives and select projects. You have to help provide knowledge and networks to move projects towards the marketplace, because the process of getting ideas to market is traditionally a very low-yield one.

HOW AWARDS ARE CHOSEN

ARPA-E awards are selected through two models: 'focused' programmes and 'open' solicitations. The focused programmes provide a unique bridge from basic science to early-stage technology. These programmes draw on the latest scientific discoveries and envision a viable path to commercial implementation through a firm grounding in the economic realities and changing dynamics of the marketplace.

The concept for a new focused programme is developed through engagement with diverse communities, including some that may not have traditionally been involved in the topic area, and by examining lessons learned from current ARPA-E projects.

By utilising open solicitations, we also ensure that we fund potentially transformational ideas outside the scope of focused programmes. Projects selected under open solicitations pursue novel approaches to energy innovation, and work to meet technical needs not addressed by other parts of ARPA-E, the Department of Energy, or the private sector. We work to frame problem statements in ways that encourage interdisciplinary thinking and bring together diverse combinations of skills and partners that can approach energy challenges in new ways.

BRINGING STAKEHOLDERS TOGETHER

From the beginning and over the lifetime of a project, ARPA-E maps who has to be involved to help move a project to market: the regulators, the suppliers and the customers, those who define value for the technology. What do they want to know, when do they want to know it, and how long might it take them to engage? Do they need to be involved at day one or do they need to be involved at year five? And again we are looking at being catalytic and accelerative, and you can only be accelerative if you know who needs to be involved in the process. And so at ARPA-E, when we first look at an area and people say 'that is impossible', we engage a variety of stakeholders who need to be involved and help walk them from the impossible to the plausible and eventually the inevitable.

So a critical component of the ARPA-E model is hands-on engagement with awardees. Each project includes clearly defined technical and commercial milestones that awardees are required to meet. Programme directors work closely with each awardee, through regular meetings and on-site visits, to ensure that milestones are being achieved in a timely fashion. When a project is not achieving its goals, we work with the awardee to rectify the issue or, in cases where the issue cannot be corrected, we discontinue the funding for the project.

Another unique element of our model is the technology-to-market programme. The most innovative technologies in the world will only have impact if they make it to the market, which is why ARPA-E regularly asks, 'If it works, will it matter?' The technology-to-market programme provides awardees with practical training and critical business information to guide technical development and help projects succeed.

THE PATH FROM IDEA TO PRODUCT IS A TOUGH ONE

As mentioned earlier, the yield of ideas to impact in the marketplace is quite low. This is a challenge every university technology transfer office and research director at a company grapples with every day. Generally the low yield is due to not having the right team, an insufficient definition of value and/or poor execution.

Another common pitfall for research projects is waiting too long to think about what happens when the project funding is over and not fully appreciating the varied needs of the value chain and the time it takes to engage partners. Each of our projects has a 'technology-to-market plan' that maps out a preliminary path to market and is regularly refined.

HOW WE MEASURE SUCCESS

The success of ARPA-E will ultimately be measured by the impact of its projects in the marketplace as realised by commercial adoption. As the projects we fund seek to generate transformational energy technologies that do not exist today, we look at various metrics to measure progress. These metrics include meeting technical milestones, patents and publications and, most importantly, 'handoffs' for next-stage development. These include the formation of new companies and fostering public and private partnerships to ensure projects continue to move towards the market.

So, to conclude, in just a few short years, ARPA-E has established a new model for government-funded energy research that frames energy challenges to engage diverse communities to move the impossible to the plausible, thus accelerating the pace of innovation.

Cheryl Martin is deputy director of the Advanced Research Projects Agency–Energy (ARPA-E) at the US Department of Energy where she leads ARPA-E's Technology-to-Market programme, which helps breakthrough energy technologies succeed in the marketplace. Prior to joining ARPA-E, she was an executive in residence with the venture capital firm Kleiner Perkins. She also spent 20 years with Rohm and Haas Company, starting her career as a senior scientist for the company's Plastics Additives business.

THE RISE OF THE STATE INVESTMENT BANKS

Matthias Kollatz-Ahnen

State investment banks form a rather unique group, but there is no common name for them across the globe. In some countries we find (state) 'investment banks'; in others 'structural banks' or 'development banks', and, last but not least, 'promotional banks'. The mission of these banks is to deliver and implement promotional programmes of the state. So they are, in fact, 'mission-oriented' finance institutions. Promotional programmes are understood to be state support schemes not given as grants, but rather as loans, guarantees, quasi-equity or equity instruments which are more market-conforming than grants.

Other attributes or common features of the state investment banks are as follows:

- They follow a wholesale bank approach and they do not do retail business with deposits (there are a few exceptions such as in France and Italy, where the state guarantees certain interest rates for [small private] savings deposits and their repayment; schemes that were historically developed to encourage savings).

- They borrow on the markets with the rating of their state owners, usually with a small top-up on the borrowing costs of the state (in normal times around 20 basis). During the crisis, some cases show that the asset-book of the development bank also has to be considered. Where markets consider the asset-book to be stable and the approval processes of the bank demonstrate sound banking standards, the bank's rating can in some cases be better than the average rating of the shareholders. A large example of this is the European Investment Bank; a small one is the Black Sea Trade and Development Bank; a mid-sized example is the CAF, the development bank of Latin America.
- Classical areas of activity are the support of small and medium-sized companies, the financing of social housing or urban development of difficult neighbourhoods, financing of industry and technical change and of infrastructure, with a focus on environmental infrastructure such as water supply and wastewater treatment.
- In some countries, the restructuring of old industries or the development of industry in specific sectors was – and is – financed by development banks.
- They follow the state's policy agenda, which in more and more countries includes supporting innovation in energy efficiency and making projects bankable that otherwise would not be bankable.
- They can be a tool for political lending – something which was and will remain controversial. The latest in-thing is an approach where the state has the right to decide on political lending, though this should of course be separated from the bank's normal asset book and covered by a specific state guarantee, bringing decision and responsibility together.

HOW STATE INVESTMENT BANKS HAVE GROWN IN NUMBER AND SIZE

The creation of new development banks is continuing apace across the world. The most prominent example is that of the New Development Bank (Brics Bank), set up by a decision of the Brics summit in Brazil in the summer of 2014. The Brics countries (Brazil, Russia, India, China, and South Africa) decided to focus the bank on infrastructure and to pay in $10bn (in shares) to the equity of $50bn (including 40bn callable shares). After some years the equity is due to be doubled to $100bn.

Another example is the Asian Infrastructure Development Bank, in which China is very interested; examples in Europe are the French public investment bank BPI France and others in Portugal, Ireland, and the UK – countries that are new to development banks.

During the second phase of the financial crisis, after the initial 2007–2008 subprime loan crash in the US became a euro crisis, the EU countries decided to make a significant increase in the capital of the European Investment Bank (EIB) with an injection of €10bn paid in, and allowing for additional lending of €60bn to €80bn depending on the risk taken.

In his first speech as president-elect of the European commission, Jean-Claude Juncker said "that a further increase of the EIB's capital should be considered". In November 2014 he announced a new European Fund for Strategic Investments, guaranteed with public money from the EU budget and the EIB and able to mobilise €315bn over the following three years.

The importance of such banks for an economy cannot be underestimated. For example, development banks' balance sheet total in Germany (considering KfW and other public development banks) is worth more than 33 per cent of GDP and activities are still growing. In Italy, development banks' balance sheet total corresponds to up to 21 per cent of GDP, with smaller regional banks such as Finlombarda also playing a role. And a new class of banks with 10 per cent of GDP is emerging in several other countries in Europe (and globally).

Such promotional approaches, with subsidy elements delivered by the development banks, are different in different countries and can change over time, reflecting developments in the financial system, in capital markets, in the macro-conditions (for example, in an environment of high interest rates the situation for soft loans is very different from that in today's environment of very low interest rates), or changes in the perceived needs of the clients.

THE CASE OF THE EIB

As the largest development bank in Europe (and the second largest in the world, behind the Chinese Development Bank), the EIB has decided to give more emphasis to the combination of grant elements with advisory services. The new slogan of the bank is 'lending, blending, advising'.

By and large during the phase of slow and fragile recovery in Europe, the public missions we are discussing are centred around the following:

- access to finance (which is a general problem in crisis-countries and a problem for SMEs in most other countries);
- long-term lending, mainly with big tickets (where market finance is in short supply for viable infrastructure and new infrastructure projects such as broadband); and
- stimulating innovation (where market finance is in short supply for high-risk ventures and those surrounded by uncertainty).

HOW THE EU RULES ON STATE AID ASSUMED THE PRIVATE SECTOR WOULD STEP IN

In the old days, the way countries approached increasing their industrial competitiveness was often through protecting and supporting new industries (for example, with import barriers) and by creating full competition for the mature ones. In the EU, public intervention is governed by a very different concept: that of market failure. Only where market failure is found and proven does public intervention with money seem justified. Otherwise, it is considered to damage markets and is banned by the rules on state aid.[1] Public expenditure given selectively to one company (for example, one airport) and not to all interested competitors in the EU (for example, all airports across the EU) is considered to be market deterioration if it has impact on the conditions of production and trade in other EU countries. Developing new industries or increasing the competitiveness of existing ones will, by definition, affect the conditions of trade and production. Only in exceptional cases will it be permitted by the European commission; in most cases it will be considered unjustified state aid.

What does this difference mean in practical terms? The private sector is supposed to take over very early on. The development of markets in worldwide competition belongs in the sphere of the state only in the very early phase. It moves very quickly into the sphere of the private sector – one would call this often the second or the third financing round. This abstinence of the state is of particular relevance for innovation financing.

In recent times (but before the crisis) the approach to financing was, in many cases, to assume a deep and liquid capital market, so that innovation and new industry would be financed as long as the risk-reward was appropriate. Development banks and the state intervention coming with development banks were considered as kind of superfluous. Thus, a reduction of activities was recommended. Behind this paradigm we find the assumption that the private sector is present and efficient – and more efficient than the public sector. This is also of specific relevance for innovation financing.

What we saw in reality was not very encouraging; private investment in early stage financing (venture capital) shrank rapidly during the crisis and was taken over by states in a market with an overall shrinking volume (see Figures 12.1 and 12.2).

AN EU EQUITY FUND TO PUSH FOR GROWTH

The recent discussion about creating a large EU growth fund (known as the Investment Plan for Europe)[2] highlights the fact that markets do not provide financing for all growth phases. In the analysis of Lazlo Andor, the recently departed EU commissioner for employment, social affairs and inclusion, public interventions in venture capital mitigate the lack of private capital for start-ups to some extent:

> Venture capital does not provide for the needs of existing medium-sized enterprises willing and able to expand – the so-called mid-caps. Many of these mid-caps lack access to equity investment that does not imply takeover of the company. In other words, there is a lack of investors interested in taking minority stake in medium-sized companies. Limited equity capital consequently limits the ability of these companies to borrow, invest, grow and employ.

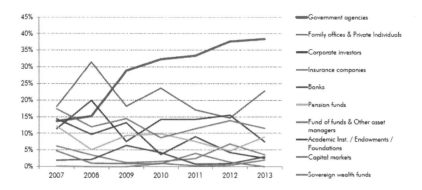

Figure 12.1. Public share in venture capital fundraising in Europe. Government agencies, some insurance companies, some pension funds, and sovereign wealth funds together form the public investment sector in venture capital. Their share now accounts for 50 per cent of venture capital fundraising in Europe. (*Source*: Kraemer-Eis, H., Lang, F., and Gvetadze, S. (2014). *European Small Business Finance Outlook*. EIF Working Paper 2014/26. EIF Research & Market Analysis. December 2014. http://www.eif.org/news_centre/publications/EIF_Working_Paper_2014_26.htm.)

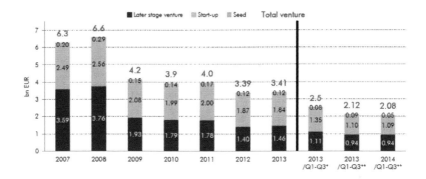

Figure 12.2. How the volume of venture capital investment declined in Europe after the 2008 crisis. Private equity shows the same pattern (less than half of the volume of 2008). (*Source*: Kraemer-Eis, H., Lang, F., and Gvetadze, S. (2014). *European Small Business Finance Outlook*. EIF Working Paper 2014/26. EIF Research & Market Analysis. December 2014. http://www.eif.org/news_centre/publications/EIF_Working_Paper_2014_26.htm.)

A 'largish' growth fund of some €10bn would unleash growth-drivers and would invest directly in such firms, based on a professional analysis. The injection to the country's own fund is paid once by member states. Once the fund is up and running, no further injection would be needed in the future due to the revolving character of the financial instrument. The investment capacity of the country reaches a higher level permanently.

The typical intermediaries entrusted by the government for such equity funds are either European financial institutions such as the European Investment Fund or specialised agencies. If such a fund is to get going quickly and be instrumental in reigniting growth, then creating a completely new EU institution should be avoided – as that would take too long to set up and for its treaties to be ratified in all member states. This situation raises a further argument in favour of entrusting an already existing and proven intermediary.

If such a fund is created, it will contribute to the growth of the system of development banks.

Matthias Kollatz-Ahnen was appointed as finance senator for the state government of Berlin in December 2014. Previously, he was senior expert at PricewaterhouseCoopers, Germany. From 2006 to 2012 he was a senior vice-president of the European Investment Bank, with responsibility for its lending programmes in Turkey, Germany, Austria, Romania and Croatia. He is a former managing director and a member of the management boards of the Investitionsbank Hessen (Hesse Investment Bank) and the Landes Treuhandstelle Hessen (the Hesse State Trust Agency).

NOTES

1. For more on the EU's rules on state aid, see http://ec.europa.eu/competition/consumers/government_aid_en.html.

2. Under Jean-Claude Juncker's plan, announced in late November 2014, the European Investment Bank and the EU budget will contribute €21bn in guarantees that will allow the EIB to raise funds in the private capital markets that can then be invested in unfunded projects. EU officials estimate the €21bn will allow the EIB to raise €60bn by issuing bonds, with that cash then invested in projects worth €315bn.

THE EUROPEAN INVESTMENT BANK: SUPPORTING INNOVATION IN EUROPE

Shiva Dustdar

The EIB is the EU's bank investing in Europe's growth. We are owned by and represent the interests of the 28 EU member states, boasting a sizeable balance sheet total of €512bn as of December 2013. We work closely with other EU institutions to implement EU policy. As the largest multilateral borrower and lender by volume, we provide finance and expertise to sound and sustainable investment projects that contribute to furthering EU policy objectives. More than 90 per cent of our activity is focused on Europe, but we also support the EU's external and development policies. We raise the bulk of our lending resources on the international capital markets through bond issues (€72bn in 2013). Our top AAA rating allows us to borrow at advantageous rates; thus, we are able to offer good terms to our clients. All the projects we finance must not only be bankable but also comply with strict economic, technical, environmental, and social standards. Our teams of more than 300 engineers and economists screen every project before, during, and after we lend. With projects in over 160 countries, we have a large impact on growth, infrastructure, and, importantly, innovation.

THE EIB'S MISSION

The EIB is a long-term investor, providing patient capital and support in good times and bad (Figure 13.1). Our activities are guided by the objectives of the Europe 2020 strategy of smart, sustainable, and inclusive growth. To achieve the goals of the strategy and further support growth and jobs in Europe, we intend to continue to support four priority areas: innovation and skills; access to finance for smaller businesses; climate action; and strategic infrastructure (Figure 13.2). The EIB, together with the European Investment Fund – the specialist arm providing SME risk-finance – strives to expand its support for SMEs in Europe even further, and has broadened the range of distribution channels and products. The EIB Group is committed to working closely with the European commission, member states, national development banks, and other stakeholders to continue to provide innovative, pragmatic, and efficient solutions to further catalyse investment in the EU and increase the leverage effect of EU budgetary resources and member state contributions.

EIB SUPPORT FOR INNOVATION AND SKILLS

We support every path to innovation. This ranges from fundamental research through to prototyping and commercialisation, as well as process innovation. We help fund the cost of researchers' salaries, research consumables, the acquisition of intellectual property rights and licenses. By financing a range of programmes and infrastructure at the EU and national level, the EIB also helps to create an environment in which the knowledge economy can thrive. Some examples include:

- public and private universities and institutes;
- incubators, science and technology parks and clusters;
- information and communication technology infrastructure, including broadband;

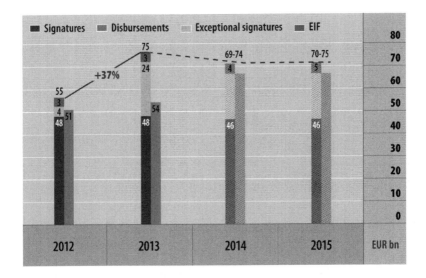

Figure 13.1. EIB's Strong Response to the Crisis (*Source:* EIB)

- promoting the adoption of innovative new technology in public and private sectors; and
- technology transfer between academia and the business sector.

HORIZON 2020 AND INNOVFIN

Horizon 2020 is one of seven flagship initiatives under the Europe 2020 ten-year growth and jobs strategy launched in 2010 to secure Europe's global competitiveness. Running over the period 2014–2020, the budget of Horizon 2020 is approximately €80bn, representing a considerable increase compared to previous programmes. Innovation can be funded not just through grant funding by the public sector, but also through innovative finance instruments like EIB's InnovFin financial products. As described by Konstantinos Arvanitopoulos, then the Greek minister of education, at the signing of the InnovFin programme in June 2014: "The new programme for research and innovation 'Horizon 2020' is one of the

Figure 13.2. Growth and Jobs: EIB's Four Key Priorities in 2013 (*Source:* EIB)

tools of the EU, expected to contribute to tackling the crisis through the development of a 'knowledge-based economy' and the strengthening of the competitive advantages of the union on a global scale."

One of the key factors constraining the implementation of research and innovation activities is the lack of available financing at acceptable terms to innovative businesses, as these types of companies or projects deal with complex products and technologies, unproven markets, and intangible assets. Under Horizon 2020, the EU and the EIB Group have joined forces to provide finance for research and innovation to entities that may otherwise struggle to access financing. This new family of financing products is called InnovFin – EU Finance for Innovators. It is a blended financing instrument combining capital from the European commission and the EIB in order to share the risk of innovative projects and companies and allow the EIB to take more risk. InnovFin aims to facilitate and accelerate access to finance for innovative businesses and other entities in Europe.

Over the next seven years InnovFin will offer a range of tailored financial products for research and innovation by small start-ups, medium and large companies, and public institutions promoting research and innovation activities. The name of the game for innovation at the EIB is to have leverage, multiplier effects, and impact.

INNOVFIN IN DETAIL

InnovFin builds on the success of the former Risk-Sharing Finance Facility, developed under the seventh EU framework programme for research and technological development (FP7). During the 2007–2013 programming period, the Risk-Sharing Finance Facility financed 114 RDI projects to the tune of €11.3bn and signed 29 guarantee contracts with a total guarantee amount of over €1.4bn. The RSFF contribution, especially in a crisis context, was particularly high. Many of the projects in the RSFF portfolio were negotiated and signed in the 2008–2009 period, a time when the volume of credit available was shrinking, the availability of long-term debt was very low, and the risk premium on lending was rising rapidly. Under the new 2014–2020 programming period, the EU and EIB Group have more than doubled their combined support for innovative firms in Europe. In addition to more financing being made available, InnovFin also offers a greater product range, as explained below.

InnovFin financing has been developed as a series of integrated and complementary financing tools, covering the entire value chain of research and innovation investment (Figure 13.3). All products are demand-driven instruments provided across all eligible sectors, countries, or regions. Firms and other entities located in EU member states and Horizon 2020–associated countries are eligible as final beneficiaries.

- **InnovFin Large Projects** delivers loans and guarantees from €25m to €300m for research and innovation projects emanating from larger firms, universities and public research organisations, research and innovation infrastructures (including innovation-enabling infrastructures), public-private partnerships, and special-purpose vehicles or projects (including those promoting first-of-a-kind, commercial-scale industrial demonstration projects).
- **InnovFin MidCap Growth Finance** offers long-term senior, subordinated, or mezzanine loans from €7.5m to €25m for

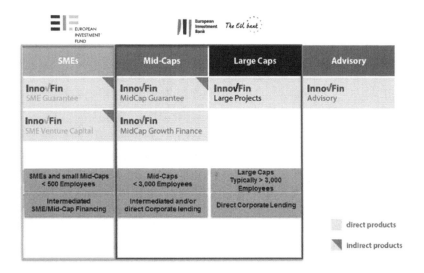

Figure 13.3. InnovFin Financial Products (*Source:* EIB)

innovative larger mid-caps (up to 3000 employees), but also small and medium enterprises and small midcaps. This is the first time EIB is systematically targeting this segment in the EU with a direct lending product.

- **InnovFin MidCap Guarantee** provides guarantees and counter-guarantees on debt financing of up to €50m in order to improve access to finance for innovative midcaps (up to 3000 employees) which are not eligible under the InnovFin SME Guarantee. This will be rolled out through financial intermediaries such as banks and other financial institutions. Under InnovFin MidCap Guarantee, financial intermediaries will be guaranteed against a portion of their potential losses by the EIB.

- **InnovFin SME Guarantee** provides guarantees and counter-guarantees on debt financing of between €25,000 and €7.5m in order to improve access to loan finance for innovative small and medium-sized enterprises and small midcaps (up to 499 employees). This facility will also be rolled out through financial intermediaries. InnovFin SME Guarantee's predecessor, the Risk Sharing Instrument, has since its inception in 2011 and until 12 June 2014 successfully supported 29 financial intermediaries in 15 countries to lend over €3bn to innovative businesses.

Under InnovFin, the EIB Group can provide (either direct or indirectly through banks and other financial institutions) from as little as €25,000 to €300m. The EIB's support is usually between 35 per cent and 50 per cent, the remainder of the financing being provided by other banks, financial institutions, and project promoters' own funds. The EIB's due diligence process involves the assessment of the company's or project's eligibility, economic viability, technological readiness, environmental soundness, and the promoter's financial situation and perspectives. Subject to the completeness of the information/documentation available and the nature of the financing, the time elapsing between a first contact with the EIB and the signature of a financing contract will typically vary between three and six months.

THE ROLE OF INNOVFIN ADVISORY

Unfortunately, there are not always enough good projects that are actually ready for financing; moreover, past experience has demonstrated that many research and innovation projects face difficulties in securing access to finance, although their fundamentals are good. Designed to act as a complementary tool in tandem with Horizon 2020 financial instruments, InnovFin Advisory Services advises its clients on how to structure their research and innovation projects in order to improve their access to finance. The service helps them to capitalise on their good fundamentals and adjust elements such as governance, funding sources, financing structure, and so on, in order to improve their access to finance and, eventually, their chances of being implemented.

The service aims to improve the bankability and investment-readiness of complex projects that require substantial, long-term investments. It also provides advice to improve the investment conditions for access to risk finance for research, development and innovation (RDI) through horizontal activities such as developing a 'business case' for new financing mechanisms and preparing studies on increasing effectiveness of financial instruments to address specific RDI needs.

One of InnovFin Advisory's assignments was the development of a new tool to direct innovative companies to InnovFin products. The tool is an application, which through a series of questions and eligibility checks provides tailored information on the products available for each request of financing (for both direct and intermediated products). Innovative companies of all sizes are encouraged to use it; however, for companies that are not considered eligible under the InnovFin criteria, relevant information is also provided on the EIB intermediated credit lines. The tool is not a credit application – instead, it is merely informative. In addition, via the request forms of midcap growth and large projects, it puts companies directly in contact with the EIB for a follow-up of their request (see the EIB InnovFin web tool address: http://www.eib.org/products/helpingyouinnovate/index.htm).

LOOKING AHEAD

The EIB continues, alongside its traditional lending, to devote significant efforts to support new initiatives, enabling innovative solutions as well as deploying more targeted products to address the varying needs of the EU member states. Currently, the EU lags behind its global competitors in private and public investment in research and innovation. Innovation is a key ingredient for driving sustainable growth, creating jobs and ensuring Europe's long-term competitiveness. That is why the EIB Group and the European commission have made it a top priority to facilitate access to finance for innovative businesses throughout Europe. We are helping to do more with less, by mobilising investment from other parties for the benefit of innovation across Europe.

Increased lending volumes will go hand-in-hand with enhanced project monitoring and expanded advisory programmes to further improve lending impact. The Bank's organisation and processes are being adjusted to be fit for purpose. EIB's holistic and proactive approach to risk management through the close interaction of risk, return, capital and liquidity will be maintained.

Shiva Dustdar is head of research, development and innovation advisory at the European Investment Bank, Luxembourg. She was previously in its risk management directorate and then in its EU lending directorate, where she was responsible for the financing of R&D projects using the Risk Sharing Finance Facility. Before joining the EIB in 2003, she worked at Fitch Ratings as director of high yield, and from 1993 to 1999 at J.P. Morgan in its M&A Advisory team in New York as well as in its Investment Banking Group in London.

THE STATE AS VENTURE CAPITALIST: THE CASE OF THE DANISH GROWTH FUND

Christian Motzfeldt

When the Danish Growth Fund (DFG) launched a new strategy for supporting the venture capital market in 2001, the diagnosis was that the Danish venture capital market was underdeveloped, unprofitable, and too addicted to soft government support. The funds were too small, too many, and too addicted to asymmetric profit-sharing schemes, all of which led to poor returns – both private and socioeconomic.[1] To establish a self-sustainable ecosystem, a more virtuous cycle was needed.

Chasing job creation, innovation, and overall growth in the economy, this diagnosis raised the question of how to calibrate government support for a future venture capital market. The DGF chose to follow an interventionist strategy based on three basic principles: ecosystem building, market-based thinking, and leverage of private capacity.

Over the last 15 years, the DGF has followed this strategy, and succeeded in supporting the Danish venture capital market to such an extent that the market now is 'number one' in Europe when it comes to early investment levels per GDP. Many indicators show signs of a maturing market with larger funds, more experienced venture capitalists, and better performing companies, leading to better returns and greater socioeconomic effects.

ABOUT THE DANISH GROWTH FUND

The Danish Growth Fund is a sovereign (government-backed) investment fund that contributes to innovation and growth in Denmark through the co-financing of high-risk and knowledge-based small and medium-sized enterprises (SMEs). The fund:

* has a focus on profitable growth in companies;
* was established in 1992 and is regulated by law, with an autonomous board of directors;
* has $2bn capital under management;
* is one of the largest Danish investors in SMEs;
* uses both equity and loan instruments leveraging private investors;
* advises government in building a risk capital ecosystem; and
* annually co-finances 500–800 SMEs.

BUILDING A SUSTAINABLE ECOSYSTEM

To establish a self-sustainable ecosystem, the DGF needed to create a virtuous cycle of larger funds with stronger and more experienced management teams who were able to find and develop high-performing companies and support them towards successful exits – thereby creating better return to the investors. To reach this end, there was a need for the government not only to engage in the direct equity financing of companies but also to support 'experience-building' and to demonstrate the effects on the entire ecosystem.

An early assessment of the ecosystem gave both encouraging and discouraging information. Encouraging was the fact that the Danish ecosystem did have the right building blocks: world-class universities, an existing cluster of solid global companies within life sciences and information communication technology, and an entre-preneurial community, perhaps immature and fragmented, but not without potential. On the other hand, looking specifically at the private capital market, DGF saw the need for considerable improvement. Facing a lack of sufficiently experienced venture capital management teams, DGF decided to build capacity to invest directly in companies alongside the support of existing venture capital funds.

One important achievement occurred in 2007, when the incubated investment managers and part of DGF's own portfolio of investee companies were spun out of DGF to become a private venture capital fund, Sunstone Capital. Today, Sunstone Capital has approximately €700m in funds under management distributed across seven funds. This makes Sunstone Capital one of the leading and most active independent venture capital investors in the Nordic market. Not all efforts along the way have enjoyed the same amount of success, though.

Building a self-sustainable ecosystem requires not only ongoing courage for experiments but also close attention to failures. This was particularly obvious when, due to lack of commercial performance in 2008, DGF had to shut down a co-investment scheme with business angels.

Over time, DGF has increasingly been financing the venture capital market as a fund and fund-of-funds investor. This has only been possible due to the patient build-up of private management capacity. In total, DGF has a market share of 31 per cent of all investments made by Danish venture funds, and in many funds it is still considered a cornerstone investor.

At present, DGF only has a small venture team making direct investments in four to six new companies per year. The strategy is to test a 'venture light' model of smaller investments in companies with growth potential that fall outside the radar of private venture capitalists. The overall aim of this activity is still the same, though: to take a leading role in testing and creating new business areas, with private investors stepping in once the opportunities become clearer.

LEVERAGING PRIVATE CAPACITY

The strategic principle of leverage implies that DGF seeks to coop-
erate with and leverage private investors whenever possible. This is
done across all DGF's different instruments. In a sense, leverage
can be seen as a necessary but not sufficient means to reach the aim
of building a sustainable ecosystem. It is only by leveraging more
and more private capacity along the way that the public agent can
make itself obsolete in the end.

Of course, a major challenge in many countries is that the existing structures of the private market are too weak to leverage; either
because no private specialised agents at venture capital fund level
are at hand or because the government is the only investor willing to
put money in an alternative asset class with, at best, varying historic
performance.

Based on this principle, DGF had an important success in 2011,
when a new fund-of-funds (FOF) was established with a capital
base of $1bn. This new FOF vehicle came to life at a critical time
after the financial crisis, making it very difficult for European venture funds to raise capital. The entire capital of the FOF stems from
Danish pension funds. One quarter of the capital is invested directly
into the FOF vehicle by the pension funds, and the remaining three
quarters is provided as a loan to DGF, who invest it for equity into
the FOF vehicle. This essentially creates two asset classes and alle-
viates the risk-based funding requirements of pension funds. The
aim is to create more growth companies as well as delivering competitive, double-digit returns to the investors.

MARKET-BASED THINKING

Support for the venture capital market comes in many shapes and
colours. For example, it is still widely discussed whether asymmetric profit sharing is necessary to attract private investors, and practices vary greatly across Europe. The private market often prefers

asymmetric solutions, while governments increasingly prefer the opposite.

DGF's new strategy of 2001 also included the introduction of market-based thinking. As a crucial first step, all prior subsidy schemes were stopped. Instead, the ambition was – and is still – to let DGF operate on a commercial basis with the purpose of ensuring the development of a self-sustaining venture capital market in the long term. Hence, DGF makes all investments – both in funds and in companies – on a *pari passu* basis. In effect, this means that future profits will return to DGF on equal terms with our private partners, thus enabling DGF to make more investments and to build the ecosystem.

Another reason for applying this principle is due to its assumed effect on the ecosystem. We argue that a government agency which minimises distortion in the private market, via either the absence of downside protection or asymmetric profit sharing, will make the private agents in the ecosystem more disciplined and the system more selective than otherwise. Hard money equals harder funds and management teams, which again equals professionally run companies. All other things being equal, this should raise the probability of a sustainable ecosystem in the end.

WHAT THE CRITICS SAY

Such a strategy is not without its downsides. Apart from the apparent challenge of investing in the right companies and funds, any public agent choosing to operate on a commercial basis will most likely face severe public criticism. This has also been the case for DGF. This criticism falls into two broad categories. First, there are critics who – *a priori* – will not accept that a public agency can make the right commercial decisions, or, for that matter, that it can stay clear of political rent-seeking. Such critics either believe that all bureaucracy is incompetent or have an inherent ideological scepticism towards the public sector doing public stuff in a private way. Second, there are critics who prefer government agencies to have a risk appetite beyond the actual course of the public agency. In part, these critics are fuelled by the belief that market-based thinking implies that the public agency rejects investment opportunities on commercial grounds on a daily basis. Such decisions can of course be difficult to accept where the decision-maker is associated with public money. Therefore, this group of critics – whether rejected or not – tend to emphasise that any 'sober' public agency should focus on subsidising high-risk projects and nothing else.

THE NEED FOR POLITICAL FREEDOM

Consequently, such a strategy is only advisable when high degrees of political freedom can be maintained by the public agency. Being a public agency but thinking and behaving as a private investor implies taking a very selective role. In the absence of a mature private market and without a track record of positive returns, only the government agency can ensure the important selection mechanism, whereby investments are rejected on commercial grounds on a daily basis.

It is crucial that politicians avoid the temptation of 'stop-go-policies', even when criticism gets bolder or when results from the early vintages of the ecosystem do not impress. Building a sustainable venture capital market can only be achieved through a very patient and long-term effort.

Following market-based thinking does not, however, imply that a viable ecosystem for risk-financing can flourish without any public subsidy schemes. The need for so-called 'soft money' is obvious, both when supporting public R&D and when bringing early-stage companies closer to the market. It is, indeed, no easy task to calibrate the supply and demand of both capital and companies across the infamous valley of death (see Figure 14.1).

We believe that it is wrong to simply increase the supply of potential growth companies by providing too many generous schemes in the early stages and at the same time neglect the support of the later-stage private market. Such a scenario, without a capital

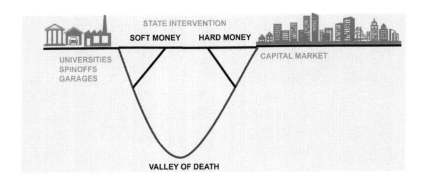

Figure 14.1. Balance Supply and Demand (*Source*: DGF)

market ready for picking up companies, often leads to a significant waste of public money. Not to forget the frustration from entrepreneurs caught in the valley of death, where too many new companies chase too little venture capital in the private market.

Any actual cluster of national policies should, of course, bear in mind their specific national context, but we prefer to let the soft money ensure that the VC funds on the right side of the bridge are incentivised to fund the best companies from further across the bridge. This gives DGF and the Danish ecosystem a technology pull character, rather than a technology push one.

MEASURING THE EFFECTS – HOW FAR FROM A SELF-SUSTAINABLE ECOSYSTEM?

Over the last 15 years we have witnessed the realisation of a more virtuous cycle in the Danish market; a cycle of fewer venture capital funds with more capital under management per fund, the highest venture capital investment level compared to GDP in Europe[2] and more experienced managers – all of which have led to a significant increase in the Danish venture capital funds' returns.

Accordingly, investments made in the period 2005–2009 have created significantly higher returns than investments made in the period 2000–2004 (see Figure 14.2).

Venture capital funds' returns largely reflect how their portfolio companies develop – and the growth rates of the Danish venture-capital-backed companies confirm the positive market trends (Figure 14.2). Sales and export growth rates among the latter generation (2005–2009) are more than double that of the earlier generation of venture-backed companies (2000–2004). In addition, job creation is larger among the latter generation (Figure 14.2). Moreover, we see lower failure rates among the latter generation; this underlines that the fund managers have become better at screening, selecting, and developing their portfolio companies – while Danish entrepreneurs have also become better at creating value.

Support for the venture capital market requires great stamina and a long-term horizon, as evidence shows that it takes decades – rather than years – to establish a self-sustaining market.

To date, DGF has had a total net loss on its fund-of-fund venture capital investments of €100m. However, there is evidence that paying the learning cost has resulted in the necessary experience of building in the Danish market. Hence, the losses occurred at the beginning of the last decade, when the Danish venture capital market was still at its initial stages, while investments made in the later

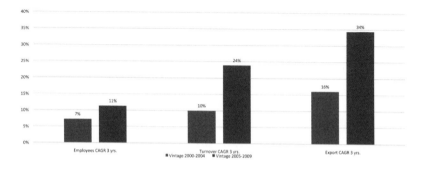

Figure 14.2. Growth Rates Three Years from Initial Venture Capital Investment in Danish Venture-Backed Companies (*Source*: DGF)

	TVPI	Net loss/gain, Million EUR
Investments in 2000-04	0.71	-106
Investments in 2005-09	1.04	5

Figure 14.3. DGF's Return on Venture Capital Investments (*Source*: DGF)

period (2005–2009) have given rise to a small surplus to DGF (Figure 14.3).

It is important to stress that these numbers only serve as a preliminary validation of the success of the above strategy. Only when, and if, the performance of companies, funds, and the DGF together and continuously show positive returns will the case for the strategic principles have proved itself. And only then will both private and socioeconomic benefits become real.

The good news is that DGF expects to see the positive developments continue and materialise in greater returns. Even though it is still too early to say whether the next generation of investments will effectively demonstrate the anticipated effect, DGF's analyses show some of the positive trends that are crucial for venture capital funds' success: more investments (especially at the early stages), more capital invested per company, and a historical high level of exits.

Christian Motzfeldt is the chief executive officer at the Danish Growth Fund (Vækstfonden). Before this, he served in the Danish Ministry of Industry and Trade, where his last position was that of deputy permanent secretary in charge of business economics. Prior to 1994, he worked at Danske Bank, the Danish national bank, and the European commission.

NOTES

1. The changes in DGF's strategy was based on a thorough analysis of the pros and cons for a market based support of the VC market made by the

Ministry of Business Affairs in 2000: *Danmark som foregangsland – innovationsfinansiering*.

2. According to EVCA data.

FINANCING INNOVATION: LESSONS FROM INNOVATE UK

Iain Gray

My contribution to this debate derives from the fact that I was until recently chief executive of an agency that, for the seven years since it was set up, has been working in just this area: investing public funds in innovation. At Innovate UK we are not so much theorists as practitioners: this is what we do, and this is what we know makes a difference.

Innovate UK, the new name for the Technology Strategy Board, is the UK's innovation agency. Our job is to accelerate economic growth by stimulating business-led innovation. One way we do this is through funding: since 2007, we have enabled investment in innovation projects in industry to the tune of about £3bn, when you include partner funding. We also do it through partnerships with all the right people. We partner with the government, UK universities, and thousands of businesses, large and small. We make those critical connections that help businesses on the journey from concept to commercialisation.

THE NEED TO BE MISSION-LED:
WHY 'TECHNOLOGY PUSH' IS NOT ENOUGH

From early on, as an organisation we have been about much more than just addressing market failures. We realised that the major challenges that our society faces – from global warming to the effects of an ageing population, to uncertainty about future energy supplies – require innovation so we can tackle them. We also realised early on that if the response can be properly mobilised, these major challenges can be a powerful spur for innovation and thus for economic growth.

In other words, we understood that 'technology push' was not always the most effective way to get economic growth. Instead, many of our programmes concentrate on the areas where technology would find application as products or services (you might call them markets), seek to identify and clarify the needs of those areas, and then work with companies who could develop products and services that address those needs. This should lead to faster and more efficient economic growth. Also, given that many of the bigger markets are in challenge areas where society looks to government to lead (health, energy, food, buildings and transport), our status as a government agency enables us to understand the policy goals of the relevant government departments and translate them into 'business English', helping those companies we support understand the opportunities.

We have also been working closely with our European colleagues, and are pleased to see that the new European funding programme, Horizon 2020, also focuses explicitly on using societal challenges as a driver of innovation.

THE PROBLEM SPACE: THIS IS ABOUT
MORE THAN FUNDING

So for these big questions – which we could call missions – we know that innovation cannot be left entirely to the market. We have seen that markets are not well-placed to bring innovation to the fore as fast as is needed. There are many reasons for this:

- Concerted action involving many players at once does not happen naturally.
- Longer-term trends are not visible to all players: for example, often businesses and researchers cannot see the nature of the opportunities and effects of the emerging technologies and policies needed to tackle challenges.
- Business investment is often too little and too late, constrained by technical and financial risks and lack of access to capital. With a major challenge requiring disruptive solutions (only some of which may succeed in the market), the risk is even greater.
- New solutions may require whole new supply chains and business models, which no one company can create on its own. New supply chains need new partnerships, and investment and innovation are required at multiple points. There are challenges in attempting to co-ordinate these major systems.

Because of these problems, finding innovative solutions often takes strong collaboration between researchers, policymakers and businesses. However, this does not happen on its own; somebody has to convene it, and often, that somebody is us. We believe that the government has a role in coordinating and stimulating innovation in complex systems and we support 'mission-oriented' approaches. We see ourselves as part of the solution, helping to convene multiple stakeholders in complex systems, and tackling innovation bottlenecks.

THE ROLE OF 'INNOVATION PLATFORMS'

One way in which we try to bring the right people together is through the model of 'innovation platforms' that we have developed. An innovation platform is an approach to innovation which brings together the public and private sectors to work on a societal challenge, where government action creates global business opportunity, and creating the right innovation programmes helps UK business to address that opportunity.

We now have innovation platforms in areas including low-carbon vehicles, assisted living, low-impact buildings, sustainable agriculture and food, and stratified medicine.

For example, our innovation platform in stratified medicine was the culmination of discussions with people in all corners of the healthcare industry, most of whom became partners in the platform. Stratified medicine is about accurately matching the precise nature of a disease with the makeup of the patient and then selecting the right therapy. The history of the UK pharmaceutical industry means that we have great capability on the therapy side, but industry capability in diagnostics could be better. Diagnostics are also multi-disciplinary: to describe the target, you need a good understanding of molecular biology, but measuring the state of that target takes advanced sensor technology and data analysis. So bringing people together is essential and can accelerate development – and this is what we can uniquely do as an arm's length government body.

There is an important principle here of how funding works alongside other drivers of innovation: in the UK, for example, the challenges of creating low-carbon vehicles or low-carbon homes have been very much influenced by government regulation, as well as public-sector funding.

There are also many other areas we work in that are challenge-led or mission-led. Our 'energy catalyst', for example, offers funding to innovative SMEs and researchers to develop solutions to identified challenges in the energy sector. Another example is the Small Business Research Initiative (SBRI), which uses the power of business innovation to solve specific public sector challenges, whether that is finding new ways of combating online identity fraud or fighting infection in hospitals.

FROM 'PICKING WINNERS' TO PICKING RACES

We do not have the power of a DARPA (the US Defense Advanced Research Projects Agency): we cannot create a market from scratch through procurement. But it is true that many of our funding pro- grammes do involve a kind of 'picking'. We do not pick winners in terms of individual businesses, but we do pick our races: the areas where we think innovation funding should focus.

A lot of factors shape that choice. We think about the areas where the UK has existing capability; where there is a global market opportunity; and where public funding can make a real difference and have an effect that could not be achieved otherwise. Govern- ment also contributes to this thinking regarding where the most important challenges are.

At the highest level in the UK the government has its overall industrial strategy, with specific elements targeted at individual sec- tors. Each strategy details the area it covers and the current and projected impact on the UK economy and tries to anticipate the developing needs of the 'market' that the sector serves. An example is the agritech strategy, which addresses the challenge of feeding a growing population without damaging our natural environment.

As you would expect, innovation is a key component of many of these strategies. Each strategy was developed through consultation and partnerships and we took part in many of those consultations.

The SBRI programme also uses challenges articulated by the government to stimulate innovation, as public bodies invite compa- nies to respond with solutions and, in the process, become 'lead customers'. Up to July 2014, 158 SBRI competitions have been run in partnership with 59 public sector organisations, resulting in contracts worth over £189m.

An adventurous recent development is to also give the public a role in the 'picking'. Together with NESTA and the BBC, in May 2014 we launched a new Longitude Prize, 300 years on from the original.[1] From a shortlist of six, the public chose the challenge of responding to the problem of drug-resistant bacteria. There will be a prize fund of up to £10m to follow up on this choice and encourage innovations in this area. That is not a lot of money in the context of drug-company R&D budgets, but setting it as a challenge is what will make it really interesting. Moreover, the other candidate areas that did not win – such as improving water supply, countering paralysis and supporting low-emission flight – are still likely to benefit from the 'challenge effect'.

TACKLING CHALLENGES THROUGH DEMONSTRATORS

One approach we have found very valuable in tackling some of these challenges is setting real-world demonstrators at large scale; this can create a major step forward. Demonstrator programmes can be a spur to accelerate innovation, align public/private funding, create collaborations, generate momentum to start rebuilding supply chains and, importantly, build business and public confidence in the technology.

A great example was the ultra-low carbon vehicles demonstrator, which started in 2010 and was the largest trial of its type in Europe. It put 340 vehicles from a wide range of manufacturers on the road, in real-life conditions, for two years. The result was a huge amount of data showing that people really would find electric cars a realistic daily proposition, building confidence in the manufacturers and the market.

Another was 'Retrofit for the Future', which used 87 projects around the UK to show how existing houses can be made much better in terms of environmental performance, potentially helping industry tap into a market of hundreds of thousands of socially provided homes.

EVALUATING IMPACT

As you would expect, a key concern of ours is how we can assess the impact of our support for innovation. Last year we set up an in-house economics capability to lead on evaluation. We commission independent researchers to estimate the impact of our activities, and through this work we know we make a real difference to UK business and the UK economy. For every £1 we invest in our programmes, we see an increase of up to £9 in the value of the UK economy, and we see new, high-value jobs being created. This is only the direct impact on those businesses we support; the nature of the innovative projects those business conduct means we would expect to see additional benefits spilling over to the rest of the economy, potentially doubling or tripling the impact of our investment. We also add more value not just by providing money but also through our networking, facilitating and wider support through programmes such as the innovation platforms. Responding to an independent survey on the Low-Carbon Vehicles Innovation Platform, the businesses involved expected the programme, which cost us £60m to run, to protect up to 500,000 jobs over 10–15 years, and add value of up to £14m per project.

In conclusion, one of the main challenges for Innovate UK has always been on which priorities to focus with limited resources. But I think we have achieved a great deal with what we have, often bringing in the funding of many partners to create a greater mass and momentum, and creating some major funding programmes that can really make a difference.

We have a model that works: a challenge-led approach that delivers through the various programmes and other tools that are available to us. The model aligns societal challenges and public and private sector innovation resources to accelerate innovation and fuel economic growth, and it is a model that is scalable.

We have a budget increase in 2015–2016, which will help. We will invest in new Catapults and programmes such as a new innovation platform for energy systems. But we have much less to work with than some other innovation agencies around the world. Could we do more with more resources? Certainly. We see challenges and opportunities that we cannot address at the moment, or that we could resource more heavily with greater benefit. But we have a job to do right now and that is what we are doing.

Iain Gray was chief executive of Innovate UK (formerly the UK Technology Strategy Board) from 2007 to 2014. After joining BAE Systems as a structures engineer in 1979, he served as head of engineering, and, from 2006, managing director of Airbus UK. He is a chartered engineer, a fellow of the Royal Academy of Engineers and a fellow of the Royal Aeronautical Society. In 2007 he was awarded the Royal Aeronautical Society Gold Medal and in 2011 he was elected as a fellow of the Royal Society of Edinburgh.

NOTE

1. The original Longitude Prize was offered by the British government in 1714 to find a solution to the greatest scientific challenge of the century: how to pinpoint a ship's location at sea by knowing its longitude. The challenge was solved by watchmaker and carpenter John Harrison, who designed the chronometer, the first seafaring clock that allowed people to pinpoint their exact position at sea. It was the very first challenge prize of its kind, and the solution not only led to safer sea travel but also was the key to opening up global trade.

CONCLUSION

Beyond Market Failures: Shaping and Creating
Markets for Innovation-Led Growth

Mariana Mazzucato

Many countries around the world are seeking 'smart' innovation-
led growth and hoping that this growth can be more inclusive and
sustainable than in the past. As we have seen in the chapters of the
book, this feat requires completely rethinking the role of government and public policy in the economy, not only funding the 'rate'
of innovation but also envisioning the 'direction' of change. This
requires a new justification of government intervention that goes
beyond the usual one of 'fixing market failures'. It means having
the ability and confidence to shape and create markets, as highlighted by the path-breaking work of Karl Polanyi. And, in order to
render such growth more 'inclusive,' it requires paying attention to
the ensuing distribution of both risks and rewards.

Modern capitalism faces a number of great societal challenges,
including climate change, youth unemployment, obesity, ageing,
and rising inequality. These challenges have created a new agenda
for innovation and growth policy that require policymakers to 'think
big' about what kind of technologies and socioeconomic policies
can fulfil visionary ambitions to make growth smarter, more inclu-

sive, and sustainable (see the European commission's 'Europe 2020' strategy[1]).

Although such challenges are not strictly technological (they require behavioural and systemic changes), policymakers have much to learn from the kind of 'mission-oriented' feats that led to putting a man on the moon, or to the emergence of new general-purpose technologies such as the internet, biotechnology and nanotechnology.[2] It was such mission-oriented investments that coordinated public and private initiatives, built new networks and drove the entire techno-economic process resulting in the creation of new markets.

Achieving such missions required not only companies that were willing and able to invest in long-run areas, but also a confident 'entrepreneurial state' willing and able to take on the early, capital-intensive high-risk areas which the private sector tends to fear.[3] A state is entrepreneurial when it is able and willing to invest in areas of extreme uncertainty, courageously envisioning the direction of change across public agencies and departments. An entrepreneurial state must welcome, rather than fear, the high risk and uncertainty across the entire innovation chain (from basic research to commercialisation) and the experimentation processes required for organisational learning along the way.[4] Most importantly, an entrepreneurial state must 'think big'.

Finding a way for government to think big is not just about throwing public money at different activities; it requires visionary investments that do not simply fix markets, but actively shape and create them, as eloquently put by Polanyi: "The road to the free market was opened and kept open by an enormous increase in continuous, centrally organized and controlled interventionism."[5] John Maynard Keynes echoed this need to think big when he argued, "The important thing for government is not to do things which individuals are doing already, and to do them a little better or a little worse; but to do those things which at present are not done at all."[6]

As has been argued throughout this book, thinking big and shaping and creating markets requires a new economic framework that can justify the role of the public sector in directing change, forming the right institutional structures that can foster and adapt to change in a dynamic way. It requires a framework that justifies the catalytic role of government, its ability to transform landscapes, create and shape markets and not just fix them. It requires new indicators through which to evaluate public investments, which capture their transformational catalytic impact. It requires different insights into the organisation of government and into the distribution of risks and rewards that emerge from this kind of collective effort towards 'smart' innovation-led growth.

BEYOND MARKET FAILURES

As highlighted by Tera Allas's chapter, 'market failure theory' justifies public intervention in the economy only if it is geared towards fixing situations in which markets fail to efficiently allocate resources.[7] The market failure approach suggests that governments intervene to 'fix' markets by investing in areas with 'public goods' characteristics (such as basic research or drugs with little market potential) and by devising market mechanisms to internalise external costs (such as pollution) or external benefits (such as herd immunity).

While market failure theory provides interesting insights, it is at best useful for describing a 'steady state' scenario in which public policy aims to patch up existing trajectories provided by markets. It is less useful when policy is needed to dynamically create and shape new markets – that is, to create the kind of 'transformation' highlighted in Carlota Perez's chapter. This means it is problematic for addressing innovation and societal challenges because it cannot explain the kinds of transformative, catalytic, mission-oriented public investments that in the past created new technologies and sectors which did not exist before (such as the internet, nanotech, biotech and cleantech) and which the private sector feared.

FOUR OPPORTUNITIES FOR CHANGING THE
INNOVATION POLICY DISCOURSE

Market failure theory continues to guide policymaking today. Yet its limitations mean it cannot evaluate the potential of the state to do four crucial things:

- Set the direction of change.
- Form indicators through which to evaluate its transformational impact.
- Set up organisations in the public sector that are willing and able to welcome rather than fear failure.
- Finally, earn some return from the upside of successful innovations to fund the many inevitable failures that are part and parcel of the innovation process.

SO HOW DO THESE LIMITATIONS WORK?

First, directionality: envisioning and 'picking' strategically. Innovation has not only a rate but also a direction.[8] However, in the ambition to achieve innovation-led growth, debates about directionality are often neglected. Shale gas, which was discovered after decades of US government investment,[9] is a case in point, considering the negative impact that the technology required to produce it – fracking – has on natural environments. Therefore, public investments to address societal challenges must give particular consideration to the types of vision and directionality they embody. It is also important to consider the involvement of civil society in the debate about such directions.[10]

The importance of such a debate is absent from traditional economic policies. These aim simply to correct markets and assume that once the sources of the failure have been addressed, market forces will efficiently direct the economy to a path of growth and development. Yet markets are 'blind' and the direction of change provided by them often represents suboptimal outcomes from a societal point of view.[11] This is why, in addressing societal challenges, states have had to lead the process and provide the direction towards new 'techno-economic paradigms',[12] which do not come about spontaneously from market forces. In both the mass production revolution and the IT revolution governments made direct mission-oriented investments in the technologies that enabled these revolutions to emerge and formulated bold policies that allowed them to be fully deployed throughout the economy. As I show in my recent book, every technology that makes the iPhone 'smart' (the internet, GPS, touch-screen display and Siri) was funded directly by different public agencies (Figure C.1).[13] And even the deployment of most general-purpose technologies (from electricity to IT) was an outcome of public policy such as the use of suburbanisation policies to redirect and deploy the mass production revolution.[14]

Furthermore, in the IT revolution, and even in the emerging cleantech revolution, government not only funded the actual technologies (for example, the mainframes, the internet, wind and solar power and fuel cells) but also created a network of decentralised public and private actors (what Fred Block and Matthew Keller call a 'developmental network state'[15]). In addition, government provided early-stage funding to companies that risk-averse private finance would not, and devised special tax credits that favoured some activities more than others.[16] These facts seem to indicate that policymakers face a different kind of analytical problem: not whether to intervene or to stand back, but instead to understand how particular directions and routes can be chosen and to determine how to mobilise and manage activities that can lead to the achievement of dynamic social and technological challenges.

Second, evaluation: static versus dynamic metrics. Market failure theory has developed concrete indicators and methods to evaluate government investments which stem from the framework itself. These usually involve a cost-benefit analysis that estimates whether the benefits of public intervention compensate for the costs associated both with the market failure and the implementation of the policy (including 'government failures'). However, there is a mismatch between the intrinsically dynamic character of economic develop-

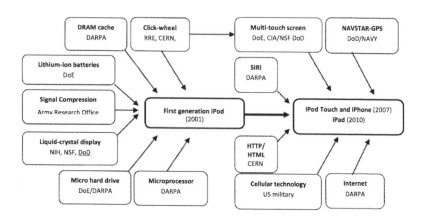

Figure C.1. State Investments Funded All of the Key Technologies Behind the iPhone (*Source:* Mazzucato (2013a), *op. cit.*, 109)

ment and the static tools used to evaluate policy. The diagnostic tools and evaluation approach based on market failure theory involve identifying the sources of market failure and targeting policy interventions to correct them. This entails *ex ante* considerations about administrative and fiscal requirements and the political and economic consequences of intervention.

Yet market failure theory provides a limited toolbox for evaluating public policies and investments that aim to address societal challenges. This is because it is a static exercise of evaluation of an intrinsically dynamic process. By not allowing for the possibility that government can transform and create new landscapes that did not exist before, the ability to measure such an impact is undermined. By ignoring the market-creating effect of public investments, analyses often resort to accusing government of 'crowding out' businesses, implying that those areas that government moves into could have been areas for business investment.[17]

Such accusations are at best defended through a 'crowding in' argument, which rests on showing how government investments create a larger pie of national output that can be shared (the savings) between private and public investors. However, this defence does not capture the fact that the goal of public investments should be not only to 'kick-start' the economy but also to choose directions which, as Keynes wrote, "do those things which at present are not done at all". By not having indicators for such transformative action, the market failure theory toolbox affects the government's ability to know whether it is simply operating in existing spaces or whether it is making new things happen that would not have happened anyway (its 'additionality'). This often leads to investments that are too narrow or directed within the confines of the boundaries set by business practices of the prevailing techno-economic paradigm.

Third, organisation: learning, experimentation and self-discovery. Taken to its extreme, as illustrated by 'public choice theory', market failure theory calls for the state to intervene in the economy as little as possible, in order to minimise the risk of 'government failure' (for example, 'crowding out', cronyism and corruption). This view requires a structure that insulates the public sector from the private sector (to avoid issues such as agency capture) and has resulted in the current trend of 'outsourcing'. Outsourcing often rids government of the knowledge capacities and capabilities (for example, around IT) that are necessary for managing change. Studies have examined the influence of outsourcing on the ability of public institutions to attract top-level talent with the relevant knowledge and skills to manage transformative mission-oriented policies.[18] Without such talent and expertise, the state loses its 'absorptive capacity'[19] (a concept only usually applied to the private sector), making it difficult to coordinate and provide direction to private actors when formulating and implementing policies that address new technological opportunities and societal challenges. Indeed, there seems to be a self-fulfilling prophecy whereby the less mission-oriented 'big thinking' occurs in government, the less talent and expertise the public sector is able to attract, the less well it performs, and the less 'big thinking' it is allowed to do. In order to promote transformation of the economy by shaping and creating technologies, sectors and markets, the state must organise itself so that it has the 'intelligence' (or policy capacity) to think big and formulate bold policies. This does not mean it will always succeed;

indeed, the underlying uncertainty in the innovation process means that the state will often fail. However, if the emphasis is on the policymaking as a process of experimentation (as emphasised by the inspiring development economist and planner Albert Hirschman[20]) that can allow the public sector to envision and manage transformational change,[21] then it is essential to understand the appropriate structures of public organisations and their ability to build internal competencies and 'absorptive capacity'.

Fourth, risks and rewards: towards symbiotic private-public partnerships. As already highlighted, market failure theory says little about cases in which the state is the lead investor and risk-taker in capitalist economies through mission-oriented investments and policies.[22] Having a vision of which way to drive an economy requires direct and indirect investment in particular areas, from specific technologies, firms and sectors. This requires crucial choices to be made, the fruits of which will create some winners, but also many losers. Is it right that the public funds socialise the losses and allow the wins to be fully privatised? Will the returns from the successes come back to the public sector simply via taxes (paid by firms and by those earning higher incomes)?

In shaping the green agenda in the US, the Obama administration recently provided large guaranteed loans to two green-tech companies: $500m to Solyndra and $465m to Tesla Motors. While the latter is often glorified as a success story, the former failed miserably and became the latest example, used widely by both economists and the popular media, of government being unable to 'pick winners'. Indeed, the taxpayer picked up the bill and complained. Is it right that US taxpayers shouldered the Solyndra loss, yet made nothing from the Tesla profits? Or, put another way, are taxes currently bringing back enough returns to government budgets to fund high-risk investments that will probably fail?

Should the government have retained some equity in Tesla to fund the other inevitable losses it would experience (as the Solyndra experience highlights)? Economists argue that public rewards in part come through taxes collected by the state; yet the reality is that taxes are, to a large degree, evaded and avoided by companies including Apple and Google, whose algorithm was publicly funded. But even if they were not dodging tax, tax rates, such as that on capital gains, have been falling due to the prevailing narrative that it is only a narrow set of agents who are the real innovators, wealth creators and risk-takers. It is, indeed, this same narrative that has justified the increasing financialisation of the private sector, with many large companies in IT, energy and pharmaceuticals spending more of their returns on share buybacks than on R&D (as discussed by William Lazonick in his chapter in this volume).[23] Only when this limited and biased 'wealth-creation' narrative is debunked can we begin to build more 'symbiotic' innovation ecosystems that can ensure future funding by both public and private actors. Should some of the public reward for public risk-taking occur through the retention of a golden share of the patents? Or through equity? Or through income contingent loans? And/or through a major overhaul of the tax system? Regardless of the answer, the questions highlight the need to build a theoretical framework that can help the public sector understand both its 'portfolio' choices and how to socialise not only the risks of those investments but also the rewards.

In building a portfolio, it is crucial to make sure that the assumptions regarding the distribution of returns, as well as their measurement, are driven by a real understanding of the fundamental uncertainty that drives the innovation process, the collective group of actors that absorb that uncertainty through space and time, and the broad nature of 'social returns'.

CONCLUSION: A NEW FRAMEWORK REQUIRES NEW QUESTIONS

In sum, this concluding chapter has argued that to approach the innovation challenge of the future, we must open up the discussion: away from the worry about 'picking winners' and 'crowding out' towards four key questions for the future:

- **Directions**: How can public policy be understood in terms of setting the direction and route of change; that is, shaping and creating markets rather than just fixing them? What can be learned from the ways in which directions were set in the past and how can we stimulate more democratic debate about such directionality?

- **Evaluation**: How can an alternative conceptualisation of the role of the public sector in the economy to market failure theory translate into new indicators and assessment tools for evaluating public policies, beyond the microeconomic cost-benefit analysis? How does this alter the 'crowding in'/ 'crowding out' narrative?

- **Organisational change**: How should public organisations be structured so they accommodate the risk-taking and explorative capacity and the capabilities needed to envision and manage contemporary challenges?

- **Risks and rewards**: How can this alternative conceptualisation be put into practice so that it frames investment tools so that they not only socialise risk but also have potential to socialise the rewards that enable 'smart growth' to also be 'inclusive growth'?

The chapters in this book have considered these questions both directly and indirectly. By considering the need for government policy to 'transform', be catalytic, and create and shape markets and not just fix them, it is essential to reframe the key questions of economic policy from static ones (that worry about 'crowding out' and picking winners) to more dynamic ones that are constructive in forming the types of public–private interactions that can create new innovation and industrial landscapes.

In the same way that putting a man on the moon required many sectors to interact in new ways, the 'green' direction being debated today also requires a green direction in many sectors. As highlighted by Perez, green is not only about wind, solar and biofuels, but also about new engines, new maintenance systems and new ways of thinking about product obsolescence.[24] This is not about prescribing specific technologies, but providing directions of change around which bottom-up solutions can then experiment. As Andy Stirling has recently put it, "The more demanding the innovation challenges like poverty, ill health or environmental damage, the greater becomes the importance of effective policy. This is not a question of 'picking winners' – an uncertainty-shrouded dilemma which is anyhow equally shared between public, private and third sectors. Instead, it is about engaging widely across society, in order to build the most fruitful conditions for deciding what 'winning' even means."[25]

Fundamentally this book has argued that we need to begin this transformation with a more serious conversation about how to direct investments that will shape and create the kind of markets we need and want. What is the division of innovative labour between business and government to fund the technological and societal missions of the future? And, given that the market is not a bogeyman forcing short-termism, but a result of interactions and choices made by different types of public and private actors, how can we make sure each of these actors is increasing its capacity to understand and invest in future opportunities so that future missions are characterised by dynamic and symbiotic public-private partnerships?

Mariana Mazzucato holds the R.M. Phillips Chair in the Economics of Innovation at SPRU in the University of Sussex. Her recent book, *The Entrepreneurial State: Debunking Private vs. Public Sector Myths*, was featured on the 2013 Books of the Year lists of the *Financial Times* and *Forbes*, and it focuses on the need to develop new frameworks to understand the role of the state in economic growth – and how to enable rewards from innovation to be just as 'social' as the risks taken. She is winner of the 2014 New Statesman SPERI Prize in Political Economy and in 2013 the *New Republic* called her one of the "three most important thinkers about innovation". She advises the UK government and the European commission on innovation-led growth. Her research outputs, media engagement and talks (in-

cluding her TED Global talk) can be found on her website
(www.marianamazzucato.com).

NOTES

1. http://ec.europa.eu/europe2020/index_en.htm.

2. See, for example, Foray, D., Mowery, D. and Nelson, R. R. (2012)
'Public R&D and Social Challenges: What Lessons from Mission R&D
Programs?' *Research Policy,* 41(10), 1697–1902.

3. Mazzucato, M. (2013a) *The Entrepreneurial State: Debunking the
Public Vs. Private Myth in Risk and Innovation.* London: Anthem Press.

4. Hirschman, A. O. (1967) *Development Projects Observed.* Brook-
ings Institution Press; Rodrik, D. (2013) *Green Industrial Policy,* Princeton
University Working Paper.

5. Polanyi, K. (2001 [1944]). *The Great Transformation: The Political
and Economic Origins of Our Time.* 2nd ed. Beacon Paperback edn. Boston:
Beacon Press, 146.

6. Keynes, J. M. (1926) *The End of Laissez-faire.* London: Prometheus
Books.

7. Arrow, K. 'An extension of the Basic Theorems of Classical Welfare Economics'. *Second Berkeley Symposium on Mathematical Statistics
and Probability,* Berkeley: University of California Press; Bator, F. M.
(1958) 'The Anatomy of Market Failure', *Quarterly Journal of Economics,*
72(3), 351–79.

8. Stirling, A. 2009. *Direction, Distribution and Diversity! Pluralising
Progress in Innovation, Sustainability and Development.* Brighton: STEPS
Centre, University of Sussex.

9. Shellenberger, M., Nordhaus, T., Jenkins, J. & Trembath, A. (2012)
'US Government Role in Shale Gas Fracking History: An Overview and
Response to Our Critics', *The Breakthrough,* March 2. Available at http://
thebreakthrough.org/archive/shale_gas_fracking_history_and (accessed
13/7/2014).

10. Schot, J. and Geels, F. W. (2007) 'Niches in Evolutionary Theories
of Technical Change – A Critical Survey of the Literature', *Journal of
Evolutionary Economics,* 17(5), 605–22.

11. Nelson, R. R. and Winter, S. G. (1982) *An Evolutionary Theory of
Economic Change.* Cambridge (MA): Belknap Press; Dosi, G. (1982)

'Technological Paradigms and Technological Trajectories: A Suggested Interpretation of the Determinants and Directions of Technical Change', *Research Policy,* 11(3), 147–62.

12. Perez, C. (2002) *Technological Revolutions and Financial Capital: The Dynamics of Bubbles and Golden Ages.* Cheltenham, UK; Northampton, MA, USA: E. Elgar Pub.

13. Mazzucato (2013a), *op. cit.*

14. Mazzucato, M., & Perez, C. (2014), 'Innovation as Growth Policy', in *The Triple Challenge: Europe in a New Age.* J. Fagerberg, S. Laestadius, and B. Martin (eds.) Oxford: Oxford University Press, forthcoming.

15. Block, F.L., & Keller, M.R. (2011). *State of Innovation: The U.S. Government's Role in Technology Development.* Boulder, CO: Paradigm Publishers.

16. Mazzucato, M. (2013b) 'Financing innovation: Creative Destruction vs. Destructive Creation', *Industrial and Corporate Change,* 22(4), 851–67.

17. Mazzucato, M. (2014) *Building the Entrepreneurial State: A New Framework for Envisioning and Evaluating a Mission-Oriented Public Sector,* Levy Institute Working Paper no. 824.

18. Kakabadse, A. and Kakabadse, N. (2002) 'Trends in Outsourcing: Contrasting USA and Europe', *European Management Journal,* 20(2), 189–98.

19. Cohen, W. M. and Levinthal, D. A. (1990) 'Absorptive Capacity: A New Perspective on Learning and Innovation', *Administrative Science Quarterly,* 35(1).

20. Hirschman (1967), *op. cit.*; Nelson and Winter (1982), *op. cit.*

21. Rodrik (2013), *op. cit.*

22. Foray et al. (2012), *op. cit.*

23. Lazonick, W. and Mazzucato, M. (2013) 'The Risk-Reward Nexus in the Innovation-Inequality Relationship: Who Takes the Risks? Who Gets the Rewards?' *Industrial and Corporate Change,* 22(4), 1093–1128.

24. Mazzucato and Perez (2014), *op. cit.*

25. Stirling, A. (2014) 'Making Choices in the Face of Uncertainty', *Themed Annual Report of the Government Chief Scientific Adviser*, Chapter 2 (June). Draft mimeo.